THE
REDUCETARIAN
COOKBOOK

Edited by **BRIAN KATEMAN,** President and Cofounder of the Reducetarian Foundation

Recipes by **PAT CROCKER** Photographs by **ASHLEIGH AMOROSO**

Foreword by DEEPAK CHOPRA, MD
New York Times Bestselling Author

THE REDUCETARIAN COOKBOOK

125 Easy, Healthy, and Delicious

Plant-Based Recipes for

Omnivores, Vegans, and

Everyone In-Between

CENTER STREET

New York Nashville

Center Street
Hachette Book Group
1290 Avenue of the Americas, New York, NY 10104
centerstreet.com
twitter.com/centerstreet

First Edition: September 2018

Center Street is a division of Hachette Book Group, Inc. The Center Street name and logo are trademarks of Hachette Book Group, Inc.

The publisher is not responsible for websites (or their content) that are not owned by the publisher.

The Hachette Speakers Bureau provides a wide range of authors for speaking events. To find out more, go to www.HachetteSpeakersBureau.com or call (866) 376-6591.

Print book interior design by Laura Klynstra.

Library of Congress Catalog Number: 2018940992

ISBNs: 978-1-5460-8277-4 (paperback), 978-1-5460-8278-1 (ebook)

Printed in the United States of America

LSC-C

10 9 8 7 6 5 4 3 2 1

FOR ISABEL

(because you make the best
vegan chocolate chip cake)

FOR MOM AND DAD

(because you once bribed me
with a quarter to try broccoli)

—BRIAN KATEMAN

Cocoa Energy Bars, page 49

CONTENTS

GRAINS AND SIDES

MAINS AND CORE MEALS

DESSERTS AND SWEET TREATS

Quinoa Power Bowl with
Cauliflower and Chickpeas, page 94

FOREWORD

by Deepak Chopra

At this moment we are witnessing a seismic shift in how people are fueling their bodies. It can be sensed from the headlines. Last year, reality television personality Kylie Jenner announced via social media platform Snapchat that she had adopted a vegan diet and joined celebrities like Miley Cyrus, Beyoncé, and Ellen DeGeneres and notable politicians like Cory Booker and Al Gore in touting the benefits of cutting back on animal products. Even athletes are jumping on the plant-based bandwagon. Football quarterback Tom Brady recently teamed up with vegan-food supplier Purple Carrot to launch a new meal-delivery service designed to help active individuals stay at their peak; Novak Djokovic debuted the vegan restaurant Eqvita in Monte Carlo, where the tennis star lives full-time.

On another front, an extensive study found that reducing meat consumption would improve human health, decrease greenhouse gas emissions, and lower health-care costs significantly. Perhaps then it's no surprise that more and more people are becoming vegetarian. Now 6 percent of US consumers claim to be vegan, up from just 1 percent in 2014.

As I detail in my book *What Are You Hungry For?*, I got swept up in the groundswell about a decade ago. Despite the fact that I had medical training, motivation, reasonably good habits, and access to any food that I wanted, I had become a statistic, joining the two-thirds of people who are either overweight or obese. Rather than going on a deprivation diet—

which countless studies show to be futile—I decided to pursue "awareness eating," implementing incremental steps that made me feel good and were good for my body and mind. In addition to cutting back on processed foods, white sugar, and salt, I significantly increased the amount of fresh fruits, vegetables, and whole grains in my diet. In essence, I embraced a "reducetarian" lifestyle—eating fewer animal products, including red meat, poultry, seafood, eggs, and dairy. The benefits were nearly instantaneous: I quickly dropped nineteen pounds. My body felt light and energized. My mind felt sharper than ever before.

That is why I am so grateful that *The Reducetarian Cookbook* exists. Rather than repeating the same advice about healthy eating that has existed for decades, Brian Kateman's book provides you with the no-nonsense tools necessary to transform your good intentions into actionable results. It focuses on progress, not on perfection, and will help you discover the small but significant lifestyle changes that activate the body's innate ability to thrive. These teachings focus *not* on restriction but on choice—a necessary ingredient for finding joy in any moment in time. And, of course, along the way you'll encounter countless healthy and delicious plant-based recipes that are good for you and good for the planet.

May your reducetarian journey be filled with compassion and light.

Raspberry Cookie
Smoothie Bowl, page 63

INTRODUCTION

by Brian Kateman

Welcome to *The Reducetarian Cookbook*! This book—with its unapologetic practicality and simplicity—is what I wish I'd had when I started my reducetarian journey several years ago. Its mission is simple: to show you how realistic, affordable, varied, and, most importantly, delicious plant-based meals can be.

My previous book, *The Reducetarian Solution*, inspired *The Reducetarian Cookbook*. *The Reducetarian Solution* is the "why" of the reducetarian lifestyle. It presents more than seventy original essays from influential thinkers on why the simple act of cutting back on animal-product consumption can transform people's lives and benefit animal life and the planet. It features contributions from such luminaries as Mark Bittman, Seth Godin, Joan Dye Gussow, Jeffrey Sachs, Bill McKibben, Naomi Oreskes, Peter Singer, and others. For a good dose of knowledge and inspiration, I encourage you to add it to your reading list.

The Reducetarian Cookbook is the perfect sequel to that "why" because it focuses on the "how." Consider it an all-access pass to an epic tour of the plant-based culinary world—with bestselling cookbook author Pat Crocker, awe-inspiring photographer Ashleigh Amoroso, and myself as your personal guides. Along the way, you'll discover cooking tips, fun facts, kitchen time-savers, stunning photos, and, of course, easy recipes for 125 mouthwatering meals that are perfect for vegans and omnivores alike.

But before we get to the recipes, I want to share how the reducetarian movement got started, as well as its main principles and philosophies.

MY JOURNEY

As I describe in *The Reducetarian Solution*, I grew up in Staten Island, one of the five boroughs of New York City. Sometimes referred to as the "forgotten borough," Staten Island isn't known for being the hippest of places. Just ask Amy Schumer's character, "Amy," who took the ride of shame on the Staten Island Ferry in Judd Apatow's movie *Trainwreck*. But growing up in Staten Island had its perks. I had access to sandy beaches, rolling hills, and lush forests—all of which were quite beautiful and rich in urban biodiversity like raccoons and robins. As a young child, I quickly fell in love with the natural world and grew eager to protect it.

By my freshman year at the College of Staten Island, I was "that guy" on campus—a card-carrying environmentalist. I urged fellow students and the faculty to join me in saving the planet. "Take shorter showers, recycle, compost, bike, and use a refillable canteen," I told everyone.

And yet, I never really thought about my food choices and their impact on the planet. Perhaps like you or someone you know, I grew up on a Standard American Diet (SAD). It's a diet high in animal products and other processed foods. For breakfast I usually had bacon, eggs, and cheese on a buttered bagel. For lunch, I'd have chicken wings, grilled cheese, fish sticks, or pizza with pepperoni. And for dinner, I typically ate spaghetti and meatballs, a steak, fried chicken cutlets, or a hamburger with french fries. Like my friends and family who had similar diets, I rarely ate fruits, vegetables, whole grains, or legumes (e.g., beans, nuts, and lentils). If I had ever encountered quinoa, I certainly didn't know how to pronounce it. SAD indeed.

Then during a single airplane flight that all started to change. While traveling from Staten Island to Montana to present undergraduate research on the environmental impact of climate change, a classmate handed me a book called *The Ethics of What We Eat: Why Our Food Choices Matter*, by Peter Singer and Jim Mason. It was an awkward moment because I was eating a cheeseburger at the time—but I persisted and read it cover to cover. Over those few hours, I learned in vivid detail how the rise in factory farming has led to cheap foods whose cost savings occur at the expense of animals, the environment, and human health. I then conducted further research on the topic, and here is a summary of my takeaways:

- With less meat, eggs, and dairy and more fruits, vegetables, whole grains, and plant-based proteins such as beans and lentils in their diets, people who eat fewer animal products live longer and healthier lives. A 2016 study conducted by Marco Springmann and his colleagues at the University of Oxford found that transitioning toward more plant-based diets that are in line with standard dietary guidelines could reduce global mortality by 6 to 10 percent. This is because eating fewer animal products reduces the prevalence of noncommunicable diseases (such as heart disease, stroke, and certain kinds of cancer) associated with high body weight and unhealthy diets.

- Eating fewer animal products is an effective way to help protect the environment. Dr. Arjen Y. Hoekstra of the University of Twente in the Netherlands found that diets consisting of fewer animal products could reduce food-related water

footprints by up to 36 percent. In a separate study, Dr. David Tilman and Michael Clark of the University of Minnesota calculated that eating more plant-based proteins could reduce greenhouse gas emissions by up to 55 percent.

- According to the Vegetarian Calculator, which uses data from the United States Department of Agriculture, the average American eats approximately two thousand land animals in his or her lifetime, leading to the suffering of over nine billion factory-farmed animals every year in the United States alone (and seventy billion worldwide). The number of sea animals killed is so high that it's difficult to estimate (it's likely in the trillions). It's pretty simple: the fewer animal products we eat, the more animals we save.

It became clear to me that eating fewer animal products had numerous and profound benefits, so it wasn't long before I decided to become a vegetarian (aspiring to be vegan), eschewing red meat, poultry, and seafood—as well as cutting back on eggs and dairy. I didn't know of any vegetarians (besides Bill Clinton and that brachiosaurus in *Jurassic Park*), let alone what they ate. But I thought, "How hard could it be?" It was challenging (in part because this book didn't exist yet!), but only at first. I quickly realized that like most people's, my food choices had been based primarily on price, convenience, and taste—not necessarily on what was good for my body or for the planet. After some trial and a lot of error, I discovered that plant-based meals could be inexpensive, easy to find or prepare, and delicious. I was happy living a life that was in line with my values and experimenting with (what felt like exotic) ingredients such as broccoli and beans. I also felt lighter and more energetic, which were added bonuses. There was one problem, though: my vegetarianism wasn't perfect.

I occasionally found myself falling off the plant-based bandwagon, eating small amounts of animal products in particularly unique and complex social situations. I remember one Thanksgiving dinner when—under pressure from my family to partake in the more traditional fare—I hesitantly placed a small piece of a drumstick next to a cornucopia of veggies on my plate. Seizing an opportunity to poke fun at her little brother, who was showing visible signs of guilt, my sister said in jest, "I thought you were a vegetarian, Brian?" I had thought I was one, too! Had I unknowingly traded in my badge of honor for a single piece of turkey? A few months later, while out to breakfast with some friends, one of them insisted I try a piece of his bacon. And I did (which I immediately regretted). Because I was a self-identifying *Jewish* vegetarian, this further complicated the matter.

Battling what could only be described as an identity crisis, I swore off the vegetarian label and went in search of one that accurately described my dietary choices. Along the way I discovered terms like *cheating vegetarian* and *lazy vegan*—both utterly negative and self-defeating, as they focused on my shortcomings rather than on my successes. More neutral terms like *semi-vegetarian*, *mostly vegetarian*, and *flexitarian* (a person who primarily eats plant-based foods but occasionally includes animal products in his or her diet) captured my eating habits at the time—but they were also static and exclusive to people who already followed a plant-based diet. I wasn't sold on any of them.

Then on a hot summer afternoon in Manhattan in 2014, my friend Tyler Alterman and I met for our weekly lunch. As we ate in a cozy, dimly lit café near my office at Columbia University, I explained my conundrum. In turn, Tyler shared that he had also been cutting down on animal products and was having similar difficulties explaining his efforts to others. It was then that we both realized there was a need for a positive and inclusive term for people like us, people who are committed to reducing the amount of animal products in their diets and who want to inspire others to do the same. After many brainstorming sessions, we finally came up with the term *reducetarian*. This is how the reducetarian movement was born.

THE REDUCETARIAN MANIFESTO

There are four main guiding principles of the reducetarian lifestyle that are useful for conversations around dietary choice and how you might think about your own journey.

1. It's not all-or-nothing.

We have a tendency to think about animal-product consumption as an all-or-nothing premise—that you're either a vegan or omnivore. But this binary is simply not true, because we make several food choices every day. I encourage you to view each meal as an opportunity. Each and every time I eat a plant-based meal, I feel joyful knowing that the meal was good for my body and for my mind, as well as kind to animals and to the planet. But please, don't be too hard on yourself if you stumble—another meal is just around the corner. Reducetarians celebrate progress, not perfection. As Voltaire said, "Perfection is the enemy of the good."

2. Incremental change is worthy of celebration.

While some people may be motivated to go vegan overnight, many others will be motivated to gradually reduce the amount of animal products in their diet. To get started, reducetarians experiment with various strategies to see what works best for them, including:

- **Meatless Mondays:** Cut out red meat, poultry, and seafood every Monday

- **Weekday Vegetarianism:** Avoid anything with a face Monday through Friday

- **Veganism Before Six (also known as the Vampire):** Eat vegan food for breakfast and lunch, and for dinner it's your choice

- **Vegetarianism:** Cut out red meat, poultry, and seafood every day

- **Veganism:** Cut out red meat, poultry, seafood, eggs, and dairy every day

A wealth of behavioral science research suggests that people who eat less meat are more likely to go vegetarian, and people who go vegetarian are more likely to go vegan. This progression roughly translates to my own experience cutting back on animal products throughout the past several years, as I now follow a vegan diet.

No matter the speed of your journey or where you end up, don't fret—carry on. Ultimately, if you make the transition at your own pace, however you define your eating style, it'll be easier to stick to in the long term.

3. All motivations matter.

Perhaps you simply enjoy eating plant-based foods or you're concerned about the link between animal-product consumption and environmental issues like biodiversity loss and climate change. Or maybe you're driven by health concerns like heart disease, cancer, diabetes, and obesity or by animal-welfare issues like the cruel treatment of animals such as cows, chickens, and fish on factory farms. Regardless, your decision to eat fewer animal products has a positive impact on all of these issues. How lucky are we that there are so many reasons to embrace a plant-based lifestyle?

4. We're all on the same team.

The reducetarian lifestyle is highly inclusive by design. It comprises vegans (no animal products) and vegetarians (no meat), as well as flexitarians and mostly vegetarians (a tiny bit of meat), semi-vegetarians (a little bit of meat), and anyone else who is reducing the amount of animal products in his or her diet. It unites the growing community of individuals who are eating more and more plant-based foods. This concept allows us to focus not on our differences but on our shared commitment to ending factory farming and to significantly reducing societal consumption of animal products. This new perspective provides everyone—not just vegans and vegetarians—with a platform to make everyday choices to eat fewer animal products, which makes huge differences in their health and in the world.

INTRODUCTION
by Pat Crocker

Working with Brian on this brilliant, honest collection of vegan recipes was challenging—many versions of mac 'n' cheese passed our lips before one was deemed worthy of the title—and at the same time deeply satisfying. I'm proud to say *The Reducetarian Cookbook* is a beautifully illustrated compilation of fun and easy vegan recipes for dishes that everyone will love and everyone can make.

Think of these beginner recipes as no-fuss, requiring a minimal number of ingredients and steps. You can prepare these dishes quickly and with ease around your busy schedule.

From time to time, you may encounter ingredients or processes that are new to you. If you haven't cooked with tempeh, miso, or legumes, don't panic! I'll explore these new foods with you gradually. All the recipes are highly adaptable, so you can tweak them to save time or to delight the wide-ranging taste buds of your family and friends. For instance, you can opt to purchase peanut sauce instead of making it from scratch or swap in a different sauce altogether if you or one of your guests has a peanut allergy. In each recipe, I'll give you specific ideas to make it work for you!

By providing a continuum of basic recipes, *The Reducetarian Cookbook* is more than a cookbook—it is a solid introduction to vegan cooking. It will seem as if you have your own personal cooking instructor with you in the kitchen, explaining and demystifying vegan cooking and making it fun at the same time.

You'll notice that many of the recipes are designed to tackle a "carnivore moment," bringing similar flavors of your favorite meaty meals in plant-based form—like Cauliflower Steaks (page 158) instead of beef steaks, for example. Other recipes rely on more traditional swaps, such as Bean and Rice Burritos (page 175) instead of chicken burritos, or Baked Squash Curry (page 174) instead of a lamb curry. Yes, you'll encounter "coasty" delights like the Breakfast Acai Bowl (page 75), but staples like French Toast (page 71) and Apple Walnut Pancakes (page 62) predominate.

Cooking is both a liberating and a libertarian activity. You make the decisions about what ingredients are used (organic, chemical-free, gluten-free, sugar-free...) and which components you buy and which you make from scratch. Pay attention to the *Try it!* and *You've Got Options* sections featured throughout—these will allow you to make the recipes your own, with instructions for homemade components and suggestions for swapping ingredients and switching up how the recipe is served.

Cooking may seem like magic, but if you can read, you can cook. The magic comes from being engaged with the process, imagining new flavor combinations, and finding different ways to serve and enjoy the plant-based foods you love. Don't be afraid to mark up the book with the genius of how you made each recipe to suit your unique taste.

Ultimately, the mission of this book is to celebrate cooking, to honor your health and the planet by using plant-based foods that heal and energize, to have fun, and to learn a little bit more about the amazing vegan choices available to all, one meal at a time. So what are you waiting for? Get into the kitchen and cook for yourself and for—or with—those you love.

Toasted Spiced Walnuts, page 42

THE REDUCE-TARIAN PANTRY AND QUICK TIPS

No matter where you are on the cooking continuum, there will always (I hope!) be new foods for you to taste, use, and enjoy. This section is intended to be a quick introduction to vegan foods that can bulk up a recipe, add a complementary flavor spike, or enrich the nutrients in vegetarian dishes.

AMAZING GRAINS

AMARANTH: A gluten-free grain with about 13 percent protein, amaranth is the only grain known to contain vitamin C. Try it with my "Dinner in a Bowl" (see page 83) recipes and in wraps, burritos, and tacos.

BARLEY: High in fiber and protein, whole-grain barley helps reduce the risk of coronary heart disease and, like all whole grains, can lower cholesterol. Its insoluble fiber helps reduce the risk of type 2 diabetes and colon cancer. Use whole-grain barley in place of rice or other whole grains in any recipe in this book.

BUCKWHEAT: It's not actually a grain—it's the seed of a fruit on a plant related to rhubarb—but buckwheat is used as a grain. It's gluten-free and high in protein, vitamins, minerals, antioxidants, and fiber. Look for buckwheat groats (the name for the seeds) whole, toasted, or untoasted, and ground as flour. This is a superfood that makes a great addition to recipes that call for other chewy whole grains, such as Quinoa Power Bowl with Cauliflower and Chickpeas (page 94).

BULGUR: Made from cracked wheat, bulgur is fast cooking because it has been parboiled. Look for red bulgur (made from red durum wheat) and add it, cooked, to wraps, burritos, salads (especially Tabbouleh, page 117), casseroles, and soups.

CHIA: What makes these grains (seeds, actually) important is their short-chain omega-3 fatty acids. They're also rich in some B vitamins, minerals, and vitamin A, as well as chlorogenic acid, caffeic acid, and flavonoids—all antioxidants. Tip: For an egg substitute, combine 1 tablespoon chia seeds with 2 tablespoons water and let it sit for 10 minutes before using.

FARRO: AKA *emmer*, it's an ancient strain of wheat resembling long, fat, pointy rice. It has a pleasant nutty taste and chewy texture, and it supplies plenty of B vitamins and fiber.

KAMUT: This large kernel is high in protein, selenium, zinc, and magnesium, and its fiber and lipids may help keep cholesterol and blood sugar levels in check.

OATS: Oats are a whole grain that are milled, steamed, heated, and cooled in a kiln to bring out a sweet nutty flavor. Once processed, the groats can be rolled to produce rolled oats, cut to produce steel-cut oats, or ground to produce oatmeal. Sometimes recipes call for "old-fashioned oats" or "oat flakes"; both terms mean "rolled oats." Oats do not contain the wheat protein gluten. Instead, oats contain a protein called *avenins*. Oats are generally considered safe for those with a gluten allergy as long as they are not grown on the same land or processed in the same facility as wheat, barley, or rye.

QUINOA: This wonder grain has become fairly well recognized due to books and the media's touting its healthy components. In addition to being gluten-free, quinoa is packed with minerals, protein, folate, and healthy fats. *Eat it!*

RICE, ARBORIO: When it comes to making the Italian dish risotto, for the very best results, I recommend that you use the Italian short-grain white rice called Arborio because it absorbs the broth and other liquids well and produces a creamy, flavorful dish.

RICE: There's a rainbow of rice out there—red, black, mahogany, long or short grain, wild (most of which is cultivated, so ignore the "wild" part). Be adventurous: try them all.

SPELT: Another species of wheat, spelt can be tolerated by some gluten-sensitive people. I love its sweet nutty flavor and that it is higher in protein (17 percent) than common wheat.

TEFF: These tiny ancient grains are white, red, and dark brown. The whole seeds are used in some seed-and-nut breads, and the ground flour is a gluten-free alternative to wheat flour. High in iron, amino acids, calcium, thiamin, vitamin C, and fiber, teff is being recommended for diabetics and people with low iron levels and to relieve PMS.

CONVENIENCE IN A CAN

There's no doubt that using canned vegetables, especially tomatoes and beans, saves cooking time. And experts tell us that vitamins and minerals remain almost as high in canned vegetables as when the fresh vegetable is peeled and cooked at home. But there has been an ongoing conversation about the safety of canned foods and concern over bisphenol A (BPA), a chemical used in the epoxy resin linings of most food and beverage cans. BPA is linked to heart disease, some cancers, diabetes, and reproductive abnormalities.

If you want the convenience of instantly adding cooked beans to a salad or wrap for the protein they provide, be sure to buy canned foods in BPA-free cans or in glass jars.

COOKING WITH HEALTHY OILS

Don't be tempted to reach for a polyunsaturated fat (olive oil, canola oil, hemp oil, or others) for cooking at high heat. The reason is that polyunsaturated fats have a low heat tolerance—they are fragile, not stable like extra-virgin coconut oil or avocado oil. So when these fats are heated past their safe limit, which is different for each but very low for most, free radicals (carcinogenic molecules) are formed.

Look for cold-pressed oil because in this process the fruit, seed, or nut is crushed or ground to a paste and the oil is forced out with a press, allowing the nutrients, color, and flavor to remain intact. Presses that use heat degrade the oil and cause nutrient loss, and if extreme heat is used in the extraction process, the oils are oxidized and turn rancid easily.

Extra-virgin oils have more nutrients and antioxidants than refined oils. Store all oils in glass containers and keep all except coconut oil in the refrigerator.

AVOCADO OIL: Consisting primarily of monounsaturated fatty acids, with some saturated and polyunsaturated, avocado oil is your best choice for cooking at medium-high to high temperatures due to its high smoke point. Its major health benefits include reducing inflammation and protecting the heart.

COCONUT OIL: For plant-based eaters, another choice (after avocado oil) for all kinds of cooking at medium to medium-high temperatures is coconut oil. Coconut oil was vilified, then reconciled, and now the American Heart Association has issued an advisory that recommends avoiding all saturated fats, so do your own research and consider using coconut oil in moderation.

FLAX OIL: Because it's high in omega-3 fatty acids, especially alpha-linolenic acid, plant-based eaters use this oil in uncooked dips, dressings, and other raw recipes to help supplement their diet.

NUT OILS: All nut oils except macadamia nut oil are rich in polyunsaturated fats, which make them a poor choice for cooking. They taste awesome, though, so use them in recipes that do not require cooking.

OLIVE OIL: A major part of the Mediterranean diet, olive oil is well known for its heart-healthy benefits—it can raise HDL cholesterol and lower LDL cholesterol. Use only medium-low to medium heat when cooking with olive oil.

TOASTED SESAME OIL: Sesame oil is available in most supermarkets, but look for toasted sesame oil because the flavor is richer than regular sesame oil. It is smoky and adds a distinctive Asian flair to foods when used in very small amounts to spike flavor (not for frying).

COOKING WITH SOY

The debate over soy has been gaining momentum in recent years, with some trumpeting the benefits of soy and others protesting against the versatile bean. Some studies have suggested that consuming soy benefits cardiovascular health and weight loss and helps prevent certain cancers. However, other studies have suggested that certain components of soy (isoflavones, which are chemically similar to estrogens) might stimulate the growth of cancer cells. So the question remains: Should you be eating soy? I say, continue to follow the research. If you decide to consume soy after weighing the pros and cons, I suggest doing so only in moderation, and for the full benefits, choose whole soy (such as steamed edamame) or fermented soy (such as miso or tempeh) and minimize your intake of highly processed soy, which is found in many packaged foods. If you are looking to avoid GMOs, choose organic soy beans and soy products.

The following are some common forms of soy that may be added to recipes:

EDAMAME: Fresh (raw), frozen, dry roasted, or steamed immature green soybeans.

SOYBEANS: Most often purchased dried, then soaked and cooked before they are added to recipes.

SOY FLOUR: Made from ground dried soybeans; may be used as a wheat substitute.

SOY MILK: A nondairy milk made from cooked soybeans.

TOFU: Solid white blocks made by pressing soy milk.

The following fermented soy products, when used in small amounts, can add flavor to vegan dishes:

MISO: Also known as miso paste, a high-protein fermented seasoning made from soybeans, cultured

CAUTION: OILS TO AVOID

Canola oil (see page 9), corn oil, cottonseed oil, grapeseed oil, rice bran oil, safflower oil, sesame oil, soybean oil, and sunflower oil are highly processed, refined products that are overrich in omega-6 fatty acids and may contain toxic trans fats.

Omega-6 fatty acids encourage inflammation, among other things, and we already get enough of them in our diet from seeds and nuts. Omega-3 fatty acids have the opposite effect as omega-6 fatty acids, so a healthy diet has a good balance of the two. But there are only a few plant-based sources of omega-3 fatty acids—the main ones are walnuts and flax and chia seeds—so to keep the intake of omega-6 and omega-3 balanced, it's important to avoid foods with excess omega-6 fatty acids, such as processed, refined foods. I don't advise using the oils listed above, except for small amounts of toasted sesame oil for flavor, because they are high in omega-6.

grains, salt, and water. Use it to add umami flavor, especially to dressings, sauces, dips, and spreads.

SOY SAUCE: A liquid pressed from a fermented paste made from soybeans, roasted grain, brine, and mold.

TAMARI: A darker, richer kind of soy sauce made with little or no wheat, making it a good choice for gluten-sensitive people.

TEMPEH: Naturally cultured and fermented, made by pressing soybeans into a cake that is usually sold frozen. I use it in Shakshuka-Style Tempeh (page 182).

HERBS AND SPICES FOR SPIKING FLAVOR

Green herbs are antioxidant, and some have anti-inflammatory power, along with a host of other health benefits, while spices offer unique medicinal effects. The following are some of the herbs and spices most often used in our recipes:

CHILE PEPPERS, HOT: High in vitamins C and A, hot chile peppers include jalapeño, cayenne, and poblano.

CHILI SAUCE: A condiment often used in Thai cooking, chili sauce is usually sweet but sometimes hot, and it relies on bell peppers and tomatoes for its flavor.

CHIPOTLES: These smoked and dried jalapeño peppers are commonly purchased canned in adobo sauce.

CINNAMON: This spice is antioxidant, anti-inflammatory, and heart protective, and it helps lower the risk of diabetes. Cinnamon is a key ingredient in desserts and *Try it!* Garam Masala Spice Blend (page 25).

CURRY SPICE BLEND: Curry may be green or red, hotly spiced or mild. It is a staple seasoning in many Asian dishes. Turmeric is a key ingredient in most curry spice blends; see *Turmeric* for health benefits. *Try it!* Curry Spice Blend recipe is on page 35.

FENUGREEK: Strange name or not, it's an amazing seed from a plant in the pea family. Its Latin name, *Trigonella*, refers to the three-sided shape of the seed. While you can add fenugreek to almost any savory dish or smoothie, it is really important for the aroma and flavor of curry blends.

GARAM MASALA SPICE BLEND: This is a sweet and lightly spiced blend that is used in many Asian and Middle Eastern dishes. Cinnamon is a key ingredient; see *Cinnamon* for health benefits. A *Try it!* Garam Masala Spice Blend recipe is on page 25.

GARLIC, FRESH: The king of herbs, garlic is an outstanding healing herb. It lowers cholesterol and blood pressure; it's antioxidant, antibiotic, and antiviral; and it offers protection from cold and flu. Eating it raw is best, but cooked fresh cloves still provide many health benefits.

GINGER, FRESH: Known for its antinausea properties, ginger also helps digestion and helps fight colds and flu. Store fresh ginger in a plastic bag on the inside of the refrigerator door, or use the grated ginger right from the jar.

HOT SAUCE: For the heat of chile peppers without the prep, there are several kinds of hot sauce such as sriracha and many brands (such as Tabasco) available. Start with a drop, taste, and add more as you like.

THYME: A strong antioxidant, thyme is high in vitamins A and C and helps soothe coughs and sore throats. Use fresh or dried leaves in any savory recipe in this book—even when the recipe doesn't call for it.

TURMERIC, GROUND OR FRESH: An essential ingredient in curry seasoning, ground turmeric comes from a plant that is related to ginger, and as with ginger, it is the root that is used. Ground turmeric is widely available, and sometimes the fresh root can be found in supermarkets and at farmers' markets. Turmeric is a powerful healer—anti-inflammatory and antioxidant, it also reduces the risk of stroke, rheumatoid arthritis, and other health problems—so use it fresh in smoothies or recipes and add the ground version to your spice rack and use it often.

NUTS AND SEEDS FOR ADDED VALUE

Nuts and seeds are great sources of protein and excellent sources of omega-3 fatty acids for healthy hearts. They are antioxidant and high in fiber, magnesium, and phosphorus, and they contribute other minerals along with vitamins.

ALMONDS: For plant-based eaters, almonds are a great source of calcium. Almonds are also high in the antioxidant vitamin E.

CASHEWS: Their contribution, in addition to protein, is iron, zinc, and magnesium—important minerals for memory.

FLAXSEED: High in omega-3 fatty acids for healthy hearts, flaxseed is antioxidant and high in fiber, magnesium, phosphorus, and selenium, as well as vitamin B_6 and iron, a nutrient that is so important for plant-based eaters to source.

PECANS: Plant-based eaters benefit from pecans' vitamin B_3 and oleic acid, a healthy fat also found in avocados.

SESAME SEEDS: Whole seeds (unlike overprocessed sesame oil) are a great source of fiber, thiamin, vitamin B_6, folate, protein, calcium, iron, magnesium, phosphorous, manganese, copper, and zinc. Add white or black seeds to any recipe in this book.

TAHINI: It's a paste made from pressing sesame seeds, and if not overprocessed, it delivers the benefits of the whole seeds. When you open the lid for the first time, some (okay, a lot) of the oil from the seeds may be floating on the top. Use a sharp knife to cut through the dense paste and work the oil back into it.

WALNUTS: Eat a handful of walnuts every day for their antioxidant power and heart-helping omega-3 fatty acids.

PUNCHING UP PROTEIN WITH LEGUMES: PEAS, BEANS, AND LENTILS

For a powerhouse of inexpensive protein, I use legumes—peas, beans, and lentils—in many recipes, and they are a staple for vegan dishes. They are also high in fiber, antioxidant vitamins, copper, folate, iron, magnesium, manganese, phosphorous, potassium, and zinc. Such a variety of dried peas, beans, and lentils exists in bulk food stores and supermarkets that you can have fun discovering different sizes, shapes, colors, textures. While it's good to have one or two types of canned cooked beans and lentils available for convenience, it is not difficult to rehydrate and cook them from the dried state (see page 96).

SUPPLEMENTING WITH SEA VEGETABLES

Everyone can benefit from eating sea vegetables because they are an excellent natural source of iodine, vitamin K, and folate. But for plant-based eaters, they are particularly important because of their generous amounts of bioavailable iron.

DULSE: Often sold as a salty snack food, dulse can be added directly to salads, grains, sides, and dinner-in-a-bowl recipes.

KOMBU, KELP, WAKAME, AND ARAME: These sea vegetables that range from brown to black in color are often available in supermarkets and whole-food stores. They are antioxidant, anti-inflammatory, and high in iodine, iron, vitamin C, vitamin K, folate, and manganese. Keep kelp flakes on the table for use as a salt substitute; add kombu to smoothies; toss wakame and arame strands over salads and add to stir-fry dishes.

NORI: This sea plant tastes like mild, salty corn. Nori is antibacterial and diuretic, and it is used to treat urinary problems, goiter, edema, and high blood pressure, among other problems. It is high in protein and rich in vitamins A, C, B$_1$, niacin, and phosphorus, and so it is an excellent addition to a plant-based diet.

To toast nori: In a small skillet, toast 1 sheet of nori over medium-high heat for 30 seconds. Flip and toast the opposite side. Use toasted sheets whole to wrap fillings for finger foods, break them into small pieces and sprinkle over salads or cooked dishes, or grind in an electric spice grinder for 1 minute or until powdered in order to add to juice.

The powder can replace sesame seeds as a coating for rice or energy bars, or use it as a topping or garnish for cooked vegetable dishes. The flavor is unique and slightly salty, so while it lends itself to savory dishes, it may also be used in some dessert recipes.

THE PLANT-BASED PANTRY

CAROB: Carob may be substituted for cocoa because of its sweet, cocoa-like flavor and dark brown appearance. It is found in the "healthy" supermarket aisle or in health food stores as a powder or as chips. While carob is caffeine- and theobromine-free, so it does not act as a stimulant, it also does not contain the antioxidants found in dark chocolate. There is no reason that plant-based eaters cannot enjoy dark chocolate and pure cocoa powder in foods, and there are many vegan milk chocolates available. Use carob for a nighttime beverage if you don't want caffeine.

CHICKPEA FLOUR: This flour is ground from dried chickpeas and is gluten-free. It's amazing because it makes pancakes, waffles, and other foods stick together (without eggs!). You can buy chickpea flour at most large supermarkets, health food stores, and some Asian markets.

COCONUT SUGAR: Derived from the sap of the coconut palm, this sweetener has the same calories and carbohydrates as granulated sugar, but because it ranks lower on the glycemic index, it may not spike your blood sugar levels in the same way as granulated sugar.

CORNMEAL: Cornmeal, corn flour, and grits are all made by grinding dried yellow or white corn. Corn flour is fine and powdery, cornmeal is not as fine, and grits are the coarsest. Polenta is a porridge-like dish that is made from cornmeal or grits.

FLOUR: Flour is a pantry staple because so many recipes call for it. Most commonly made by grinding wheat, flour is used to thicken sauce or other liquids and as the main ingredient in bread, cakes, cookies, and other baked goods. When all-purpose flour is called for, you can substitute gluten-free flour, but the product may not rise or have the same texture as one made with wheat flour because gluten forms the structure for bread and cakes and keeps them from collapsing.

Rye, spelt, buckwheat, chickpea, rice, corn, quinoa, amaranth, and almond flours are alternatives to wheat flour.

FLOUR VS. STARCH: Generally, the term *flour* refers to the powdered form of a seed or grain. Many vegetables may be processed to yield a powder that can be used to thicken sauce or other liquids, so you don't need to rely on the gluten in wheat flour for that purpose. Corn, tapioca, potato, and taro are some examples of vegetable starch that are often called *flour* because they've been ground to a powder. While vegetable "flour" or starch (mostly tapioca and cornstarch) may be included in some gluten-free grain flour blends or used on its own to thicken sauces, soups, or stews, it isn't usually substituted one-for-one for wheat flour in baked products.

NOTE: Tapioca flour and tapioca starch are the same product.

MATCHA: A quality organic matcha is made by grinding the whole green tea leaf to a fine powder, making it easy to add to juice or smoothies. It contains at least three times as many antioxidants as and more amino acids than regular tea, and it boosts metabolism.

NUTRITIONAL YEAST: Affectionately called hippie dust, 1 tablespoon of nutritional yeast packs a nutritional punch, supplying all of your body's daily requirement for vitamin B_{12}, and it's high in protein, folic acid, and fiber.[1] It's the one vegan ingredient I know of that tastes like cheese (sort of). I would describe the flavor as deliciously nutty.

SRIRACHA SAUCE: Sriracha sauce is widely used in Thai and Asian cooking; it is a type of hot sauce made from a paste of cooked hot chile peppers, vinegar, garlic, sugar, and salt. It is sweetly tangy, with a bite. There may be preservatives added to the commercial preparations. You can substitute Tabasco or other hot sauce brands for sriracha sauce in recipes.

FRUIT AND VEGETABLE 101

All about star veggies and fruits, with tips on selecting, precooking, washing, cutting, and more.

---

1   Eating a plant-based diet is one of the most healthful actions you can take, but it carries a serious risk of a vitamin B_{12} deficiency. Although plant-based diets are chock-full of other vitamins and minerals, they generally lack sufficient vitamin B_{12}. Fortunately, a vitamin B_{12} deficiency can easily be prevented. In addition to nutritional yeast, vitamin B_{12} can be found in fortified foods, like certain cereals and soy milk. Yet the simplest and most reliable way to ensure you get an adequate amount of B_{12} is to take a supplement.

ACAI BERRIES: Rich in antioxidants, acai berries are the red-purple fruit that grows on the acai palm tree. They're native to Central and South America and are mostly available frozen in North America. Use them in smoothies or substitute them for cranberries or blueberries in recipes.

APPLES: Tonic, digestive, diuretic, detoxifying, and antiseptic, apples help lower blood pressure. Eat them raw as a snack or cooked, and enjoy them as good sources of vitamins A, B, and C. Wash and peel if not organic.

ASPARAGUS: Look for straight, crisp spears with tightly closed green or purple tips. Surprisingly, fat stalks are more tender than really thin ones. I love to roast asparagus by arranging it on a rimmed baking sheet, drizzling it with extra-virgin olive oil, and roasting it for 12 to 17 minutes, or until al dente, in an oven preheated to 375°F.

Asparagus is in season in the spring, so substitute zucchini spears in other seasons of the year.

BERRIES: In general, think of berries as multivitamins in multiple flavors. They're high in vitamins A and C, which make them antioxidant; they're high in fiber, which helps to decrease appetite and increase feelings of fullness; and they are anti-inflammatory, which decreases the risk of heart disease and other health problems.

BROCCOLI: Green and good for you, broccoli is a glorious addition to wraps, burritos, soups, and stews. High in vitamins A and C, with fiber for good digestion, what's not to love? Cut the florets off the head, rinse, and steam or cook just until fork-tender. Peel the stalks, shred, and add to salads, soups, and stews.

BRUSSELS SPROUTS: Like all cruciferous vegetables (bok choy, cabbage, cauliflower, Chinese cabbage, collard greens, broccoli), these tiny, perfect cabbages grow on a stalk (a very thick stem!) and are packed with disease-fighting nutrients, including several carotenoids (beta-carotene, the precursor to vitamin A; lutein; zeaxanthin); vitamins C, E, and K; folate; and minerals. Cut them in half or, if you want to leave them whole, cut an X at the base of the stem to hasten cooking.

DAIKON RADISH: This long, white, mild-tasting tuber is high in vitamin C. I shred it for coleslaw and add it to salads and other recipes that call for shredded cabbage. The green leaves are edible.

FENNEL BULB: Slightly anise (licorice) in flavor, the white base of the stalks that form a bulb are delicious in salads and other dishes where licorice is an ingredient. The fernlike leaves can be added to sauces and sprinkled over salads.

GOJI BERRIES: Also known as wolfberries, these bright red, sweet-sour berries are eaten raw, cooked, or dried and added to salads, side dishes, and main dishes. High in vitamins C and A, zinc, iron, and fiber, they are antioxidant. Add them to salads, sides, and main dishes. Caution: Goji berries may interfere with medications; don't eat them if you have low blood sugar, low or high blood pressure, or are pregnant or breastfeeding.

MUSHROOMS: Choose firm, plump mushrooms and store them in a paper bag for up to five days in the refrigerator. Clean mushrooms with a minimum amount of water or wipe them with a clean, damp cloth. Always cook mushrooms, because raw mushrooms contain potentially toxic substances (hydrazines) that are destroyed by cooking. Look for the following healing mushrooms and include them regularly in your diet.

Maitake: Protects the liver, lowers blood pressure, protects against breast and colorectal cancers.

Shiitake: Contains immune-boosting, antitumor, anticancer, antiviral, antibacterial, cholesterol-lowering, heart-protective, and liver-protective properties.

REDUCETARIAN TOOLS

Like any other endeavor, cooking requires specialized tools—some that are essential for success and others that can be added as both your skill and love for cooking evolve.

Must-Have Tools

BAKING SHEETS: If you only buy one, make sure it is rimmed (has sides all around).

DRY MEASURING CUPS: Dry measures give a standard, accurate measure for ¼ cup, ⅓ cup, ½ cup, and 1 cup amounts. Use them to measure sugar, flour, and other grains, and any dry ingredient that you can spoon into the measure and level off with the straight edge of a knife.

LIQUID MEASURING CUPS: Liquid measures give a standard, accurate measure for liquids because you can pour juice, milk, or other liquids into the measure and read the level through the glass at eye level. Liquid measuring cups are available from 1 cup to 4 cups and higher.

MEASURING SPOONS: Like dry and liquid measures, standard spoons are used to measure small amounts of ingredients. A set of measuring spoons includes ⅛ teaspoon, ¼ teaspoon, ½ teaspoon, 1 teaspoon, and 1 tablespoon.

2 KNIVES, THE BEST YOU CAN AFFORD: Make sure you have a French knife (AKA cook's knife or chef's knife) and paring knife.

WOODEN SPOON: One wooden spoon is essential for stirring food in a saucepan because the handle won't heat up.

2 LARGE STAINLESS STEEL SPOONS: I use an 18-inch spoon for transferring food and tossing salads. A slotted spoon efficiently lifts food out of liquids when the liquid is not part of the recipe.

LARGE AND SMALL SPATULAS: Pliable (rubber or food-grade silicone) spatulas, or scrapers, allow you to clean bowls, jars, cans, and prep containers easily.

METAL SPATULA: This wide tool is used to turn or flip food as it cooks in a pan. My preference is known as a fish spatula.

CITRUS JUICER: Look for the hand tool that works by pressing the citrus half between two cups.

COLANDER: Use to drain canned goods and ingredients cooked in water or other liquids. Choose stainless steel or ceramic over plastic because boiling-hot liquids may damage plastic colanders.

FINE-MESH STRAINER: The mesh is finer than the holes in a colander, to strain out smaller bits. Choose one that is big enough to sit over a large bowl.

SET OF 2 OR 3 MIXING BOWLS: Nesting bowls are easy to store and ensure that the perfect size is always at hand.

2 STAINLESS STEEL POTS WITH LIDS: Make sure you have a saucepan, 10 or 12 inches across and 2 or 3 inches deep, and a pot, 12 or 14 inches across and 4 to 6 inches deep. While there is no single metal that is universally ideal for cooking all ingredients, start your kitchen off with the best quality stainless steel or ceramic-coated cast iron because these materials are nonreactive—they will not impart a color or taste when used with acidic ingredients such as lemon juice and vinegar.

LARGE SKILLET: If I could only have one frying pan, I would select one that is 12 inches wide and at least 2 inches deep.

SOUP POT: If you plan to make vegetable broth for soup, you will need an oversize pot that holds at least 2 gallons.

BLENDER: A blender works well when there is sufficient liquid in the jug to move the blades. Liquids always go into the blender jug first. The ingredients in our recipes are in the correct order, so follow the recipe and add ingredients as directed.

FOOD PROCESSOR: A food processor is preferred to a blender when chopping dry nuts or grinding spices, or when a mixture is dry or thick.

Nice, but Optional to Start

COOLING RACK: They're designed to cool cookies and other baked products, but I use one almost every day to cool hot pans or just to rest a dish straight from the oven. If you don't have a cooling rack, use a paper towel–lined plate for cooling cookies and hot foods, like Beer-Battered Nuggets (page 27).

MANDOLINE: A mandoline has a very sharp blade that is adjustable for different heights in order to slice vegetables to different widths. For most jobs, I opt for a handheld mandoline, mostly for salads, because it is easy to use and rinses clean. They range from small and inexpensive to larger, pricier versions. Mine is small—it fits easily into my tool drawer. Caution: Always use the food slide to protect fingers when using a mandoline.

ROLLING PIN: It's helpful for making pastry, cookie, pasta, and pizza dough; buy a rolling pin if you plan to do

some baking. They come in various materials (marble, hardwood, nonstick, glass) and with or without handles. I recommend a French rolling pin: a thin wooden cylinder with tapered ends that doesn't have handles. Or you can use a straight-sided glass bottle, filled with water, tightly capped, and chilled, for the same purpose.

WOK: I love a wok, not just for stir-fries but also for one-pot dishes where there are just too many ingredients for a skillet.

COOKING TERMS AND TECHNIQUES

Like all specialized fields of work or play, cooking has developed a lexicon of terms. Cooks use specific words and shortcuts to describe how to execute a technique or determine when a food is cooked or even how to prepare an ingredient for cooking. Some of the terms we use throughout the book are listed below.

AL DENTE: This term is borrowed from the Italian and means that the food is cooked just until done but is still firm when bitten. Usually used to describe cooked pasta, it can also apply to vegetables. To test pasta, bite into a piece; if it is cooked but still has a slight resistance, it is al dente. To test vegetables, use a knife to pierce the vegetable. If the knife goes through the flesh easily but is met with very slight resistance, it is al dente or *crisp-tender*, a term interchangeable with *al dente*.

CHUNKS: 1- or 2-inch pieces of fruits or vegetables, such as bananas, whole carrots, beans, or parsnips.

CRISP-TENDER: See *Al Dente*.

CURD: Most often used to describe a product of the cheese-making process, it is also applied to a sweet lemon dessert. Lemon curd is a thick pudding or gel that is used as a topping or to fill tarts, cakes, and pies.

DICE VS. CHOP: To *dice* means to cut fruit or vegetables into uniform cubes that could be from ¼ inch to 2 inches square. To dice round fruit/vegetables, first cut the fruit/vegetable into lengthwise slices. Stack the slices and slice in half or into thirds, lengthwise. Then cut across the stack. *Chopping* renders pieces between ½ and ¾ inches that are not all the same size or shape.

DREDGE: To coat before frying or baking. Typically, to make the coating stick to the food, it is first dragged, or *dredged*, through flour and then flopped around in beaten egg (or egg substitute, for plant-based eaters) and then dredged through bread crumbs or finely chopped nuts or oatmeal. Kids love dredging.

FINELY CHOP: To roughly cut into pieces that are between ¼ inch and ½ inch wide.

ROUGHLY CHOP: To roughly cut into pieces that are between ¾ inch and 1 inch.

SMALL DICE: Fruit or vegetables cut into ¼-inch squares. To do this, for example, with cucumber: Cut the cucumber into ¼-inch slices lengthwise. Stack 2 or 3 of the slices and cut long strips ¼-inch wide. Cut crosswise through the strips to make the ¼-inch *dice*. Repeat for remaining slices.

SOAKED NUTS: Cashews and almonds are soaked to soften them, so that they are not crunchy when blended to make creamy foods. To soak: Place nuts in a bowl or large liquid measuring cup. Cover with cool water so that they are floating. Cover and let soak at room temperature for 4 hours or in the refrigerator overnight. Drain well and use as directed in the recipe.

STOCK VS. BROTH: Stock is made using the bones and some meat of chicken, fish, beef, or lamb. Broth is made from vegetables and aromatics (herbs or spices) and is thinner and lighter than stock. For how to make Vegetable Broth, see page 125.

SWEAT: Onions are sometimes sweated to make them soft and bring out their sugars. To sweat onions: Melt 2 tablespoons extra-virgin coconut oil or avocado oil in a wide saucepan or skillet over medium heat. Add 2 cups thinly sliced or chopped onions and cook, stirring frequently, for 3 minutes. Cover, reduce heat to low, and cook, stirring once or twice, for 10 to 15 minutes, until onions are very soft.

Vegan Pie Pastry, page 195

Roasted Red Pepper Hummus, page 53

RECIPES
TOOLBOX BASICS

Basic condiments you'll use to garnish, top, or accompany many of the recipes in this book.

Baked Onion Rings, page 24

LIGHT BITES AND SNACKS

BAKED ONION RINGS

MAKES ABOUT 40 ONION RINGS

SEE PHOTOGRAPH ON PAGE 22

1 large onion, cut crosswise into ½-inch slices

½ cup nondairy milk or water

½ cup chickpea flour or all-purpose flour

2 cups finely chopped almonds or walnuts

2 cups fine bread crumbs (panko works best)

3 tablespoons Garam Masala Spice Blend, Try it! recipe (page 25) or store-bought

3 tablespoons coconut sugar (optional)

1 tablespoon kosher salt or coarsely ground sea salt, or to taste

1. Preheat oven to 400°F. Lightly oil 2 baking sheets. Separate the onion slices into rings and set aside.

2. Pour milk into a medium-sized bowl. Slowly stir in the chickpea flour using a fork or whisk until there are no lumps.

3. In a small bowl, combine nuts, bread crumbs, spice blend, and sugar (if using) and mix well. Spread about a cup of the nut mixture in a shallow dish (a pie plate works well).

4. Dip the onion rings one at a time into the chickpea batter and remove using a fork or tongs. Dredge the rings in the nut mixture to coat each side and arrange them in a single layer on the prepared baking sheets.

5. Bake for 15 minutes. Using tongs or a fork, turn each ring over and bake for another 4 to 6 minutes, until lightly brown and crispy. Sprinkle with salt while rings are still on the baking sheets. Remove rings to a cooling rack or paper towel–lined plate. Scrape any crumbs from the baking sheet and re-oil if needed.

6. Repeat steps 4 and 5 until all of the rings have been coated and baked. Let cool before eating.

YOU'VE GOT OPTIONS

- Don't like onions? Try red, green, or orange bell pepper slices instead. Delicious!

- A spice idea! Instead of Garam Masala Spice Blend, use 1 tablespoon of sweet paprika or 2 tablespoons of a combo of chopped fresh or dried herbs (like oregano, thyme, basil, rosemary, or sage). Or, if you're a hothead, add 2 teaspoons of hot mustard powder or horseradish to the milk mixture.

- Nut-free? Swap them for the same amount of oatmeal, sesame seeds, or cornmeal for crunch.

- Of course, ketchup is great with these, but why not try a *Try it!* recipe: Chipotle Dipping Sauce (page 48)?

GARAM MASALA SPICE BLEND

MAKES ½ CUP

3 tablespoons ground coriander

3 tablespoons ground cinnamon

1 tablespoon ground cumin

¼ teaspoon ground cloves

½ teaspoon sea salt

Combine the spices and salt in a small bowl. Thoroughly blend using a fork or whisk. Place in a dark-colored jar with tight-fitting lid and store in a cool cupboard.

BEER-BATTERED NUGGETS

MAKES 2 SERVINGS, EASILY DOUBLED

½ cup beer

½ cup chickpea flour (see options)

Extra-virgin avocado oil or coconut oil, for frying

1 (6-ounce) jar marinated artichoke hearts, drained

GARNISH (OPTIONAL)

1 tablespoon sesame seeds

1 teaspoon kosher salt or coarsely ground sea salt

1. Line a baking sheet or large platter with paper towels and set aside.

2. Pour beer into a medium-sized bowl. Slowly add flour, whisking constantly with a fork or whisk until the batter is smooth.

3. Add coconut oil to a deep-sided skillet over medium-high heat until, when melted, the oil reaches a depth of about 1 inch.

4. If making the garnish, mix sesame seeds and salt together in a small bowl and set aside.

5. Test the temperature of the oil using a thermometer if you have one—it should be 350°F to 375°F. Or test it by dropping a small amount of the batter into it—the batter should pop up immediately and brown on one side in less than 1 minute. (You may need to continue to adjust the heat to keep the temperature between 350°F and 375°F. This is where a thermometer comes in handy.)

6. Coat an artichoke heart by dropping it into the batter and turning it with a fork. Lift it out on the fork, shake off the excess batter, and slide it into the hot oil. Turn the nugget when it's golden brown on one side, about 30 seconds. (You can coat and fry several nuggets at a time once you get the hang of it.) Lift browned nugget(s) out of the oil using a slotted spoon or tongs. Shake off excess oil and transfer to the paper towel–lined baking sheet. Coat and fry remaining artichoke hearts.

TO SERVE

Sprinkle with salt and sesame seeds (if using) while hot. Cool before serving. (Avoid burnt tongues!)

YOU'VE GOT OPTIONS

- Chickpea flour helps to keep the batter thick in this recipe, but use all-purpose flour if that's what you have.

- Experiment with chunks of zucchini and bell pepper, whole mushrooms, or almost any vegetable—except peas!

GRILLED SKEWERED EGGPLANT

MAKES 4 SERVINGS

1 teaspoon coconut sugar

½ teaspoon ground coriander

½ teaspoon ground cumin

½ teaspoon sea salt

¼ teaspoon ground cinnamon

3 Japanese eggplants

2 tablespoons toasted sesame oil (see options)

FOR SERVING

2 cups baby spinach or shredded lettuce (optional)

1 cup Peanut Sauce, Try it! recipe (page 29) or store-bought

1. Preheat the barbecue grill or broiler. Lightly oil four wooden or metal 12-inch skewers.

2. Combine sugar, coriander, cumin, salt, and cinnamon in a small bowl. Stir to mix well and set aside.

3. Peel the eggplants and cut off both ends.

4. Halve thin eggplants lengthwise and cut larger eggplants into quarters lengthwise. Then cut into 1-inch chunks crosswise. Place in a bowl and drizzle with oil. Toss to coat. Sprinkle spice mixture evenly over and toss to coat.

5. Divide the eggplant pieces into four equal portions and thread each portion onto a skewer. Drizzle any oil and spice remaining in the bowl over the skewered eggplant.

6. Cook on the grill or on a baking sheet under the broiler for 3 minutes. Turn the skewers over and grill eggplant on the other side for 2 to 3 minutes, until browned and soft.

TO SERVE

If using spinach, divide it evenly among four plates and serve grilled eggplant, on or off the skewer, on top of the spinach. Drizzle peanut sauce over the eggplant or serve on the side.

YOU'VE GOT OPTIONS

- You can add onion quarters or whole, small tomatoes between the eggplant chunks on the skewers.

- Toasted sesame oil imparts an authentic Asian flavor, but you can use extra-virgin olive oil or avocado oil in its place.

- Serve grilled eggplant on the skewer over cooked rice or noodles and drizzle Tahini Sauce (page 32) over it.

Try it!
PEANUT SAUCE

MAKES 1 CUP

¾ cup canned coconut milk

1 tablespoon coconut nectar or rice syrup

1 tablespoon freshly squeezed lemon juice

1 tablespoon soy sauce or tamari

2 teaspoons apple cider vinegar

2 tablespoons smooth peanut butter

1 clove garlic, minced

1. Place milk, nectar, lemon juice, soy sauce, vinegar, peanut butter, and garlic in the jug of a blender. Blend on high for about 1 minute or until smooth.

2. Transfer to a saucepan and simmer over medium-low heat, stirring frequently, for 7 minutes, or until slightly thickened. Serve warm or at room temperature.

TO STORE
Peanut sauce keeps in a covered container in the refrigerator for up to 1 week.

BARLEY AND WALNUT WRAPS

MAKES 4 TO 6 WRAPS

1 cup barley (see options)

1 teaspoon sea salt

2 green onions, chopped

1 cucumber or ½ English cucumber, diced

1 red, yellow, or green bell pepper, seeded and diced

1 cup cooked black beans or chickpeas

½ cup finely shaved red or green cabbage

½ cup chopped fresh herbs (basil, thyme, parsley, mint, and dill, in any combination)

¼ cup chopped toasted walnuts

Sea salt (optional)

4 to 6 (10-inch) tortillas (see options)

½ to ¾ cup Tahini Sauce, Try it! recipe (page 32) or store-bought

1. Cook the grain: Bring 2 cups of water to a boil in a large saucepan over high heat. Stir in barley and salt and bring back to a boil. Cover, reduce heat to medium-low, and simmer for 20 minutes. At this point, test a cooled grain by chewing it. Keep cooking and checking every 10 minutes until the grain is al dente. (Don't overcook grains until they are soft or, worse, mushy.) Drain and rinse with cool water. Set aside to drain and cool completely.

2. Combine green onions, cucumber, pepper, beans, cabbage, herbs, and walnuts—or experiment with your own fillings—in a large bowl. Add cooled grains and toss to mix well. Taste and add salt if required.

3. Heat the tortillas by lightly toasting them in a skillet. (Alternatively, wrap them in tinfoil and warm for 20 minutes in a preheated 300°F oven.) Lay one tortilla on a clean work surface.

4. Use a large spoon or 1-cup measuring cup to scoop 1 cup of filling into the center of the tortilla. Drizzle about 2 tablespoons tahini sauce over the top.

5. (And now for the fun part!) Fold each end of the tortilla (top and bottom) over the filling. Then fold the right side over the filling and spin the tortilla one-quarter turn to the right. Using two hands, gently pull the covered filling toward you to make a tight roll. Roll the filled half of the tortilla away from you and over the rest of the tortilla. Secure with toothpicks if you like.

(continued)

If ever there were a totally egalitarian recipe, this is it! The recipe on page 31 is designed as a starting point for building your very own wonder wrap, and it pales to what you can dream up.

- Grains are essential in burritos and wraps, so experiment. Rice is the obvious choice, but barley (Scotch and pot barley have more of the outer husk than pearl barley), spelt, and wheat berries have a nutty flavor and a chewy texture. If using rice, it should be cooked al dente after 20 minutes, and whole wheat berries after another 40 or 50 minutes.

- Try brown rice, whole wheat, or corn tortillas.

- Vegan Bacon (page 87) adds so much flavor to wraps and is so easy to make.

Try it! TAHINI SAUCE

MAKES ABOUT ½ CUP

¼ cup tahini

2 tablespoons freshly squeezed lemon juice

2 tablespoons nondairy milk

1 or 2 cloves garlic, minced

½ teaspoon sea salt

¼ teaspoon cayenne pepper (optional)

1. Combine all ingredients in a small bowl. Mix with a whisk or fork until blended.

2. Taste, and add more lemon juice if you want a slightly thinner sauce.

TO STORE
Tahini sauce keeps in a covered container in the refrigerator for up to 1 week.

RICE NUGGETS (AKA ONIGIRI)

MAKES 16 TO 20 NUGGETS

2 tablespoons tahini

1 tablespoon Vegan Parmesan Cheese (page 39), or store-bought

2 teaspoons rice vinegar

2 teaspoons soy sauce or tamari

2 teaspoons toasted sesame oil

2 cups cooked short-grain brown or black rice

16 to 20 walnut halves or 1-inch avocado chunks

½ cup white or black sesame seeds

1. Line a baking sheet with parchment paper.

2. Combine tahini, vegan Parmesan cheese, vinegar, soy sauce, and oil in a large bowl. Whisk with a fork to mix. Add rice and toss to coat evenly (rice will be sticky). Set aside for 10 minutes.

3. Lightly oil your hands and scoop 2 tablespoons of the mixture into the palm of one hand. Place a nut in the center and roll the rice around the nut. Place nugget on prepared baking sheet. Repeat until all of the rice mixture has been formed into nuggets. (You can make nuggets one day ahead of time to this point. Cover with plastic wrap and refrigerate. When ready to finish, bring to room temperature and continue with step 4.)

4. Spread half of the sesame seeds in a shallow dish. Roll nuggets in seeds to cover them completely, adding remaining sesame seeds as required.

Note: We've called these tasty bites *nuggets*, but in Japan, you would be eating onigiri [oh-nee-gee-ree], a rice ball formed around a meat or vegetable filling and shaped into a triangle. Often onigiri are wrapped in nori (see page 13).

LENTIL SLIDERS

MAKES 8 SLIDERS OR 6 REGULAR-SIZE PATTIES   SEE PHOTOGRAPH ON COVER

1 cup dried brown or green lentils (see options)

2¼ to 2½ cups vegetable broth or water, divided

3 tablespoons extra-virgin avocado oil, divided

1 medium onion, chopped

2 cloves garlic, chopped

1 small carrot, chopped

1 teaspoon Curry Spice Blend, Try it! recipe (page 35) or store-bought

1 cup finely chopped walnuts

½ teaspoon sea salt

1 or 2 tablespoons Dijon mustard

8 small hamburger buns

GARNISH (OPTIONAL)

Ketchup, Mayonnaise, Mustard, Relish, Sliced onion, Sliced tomato

TO SERVE

Serve patties between hamburger buns and pass the condiments and toppings separately.

PAT'S TIP: Let's face it: these patties are crumbly, making it practical to eat them with a fork—but they are so delicious, and we love them!

1. Preheat oven to 375°F. Line a baking sheet with parchment paper.

2. Combine lentils and 2 cups of the broth in a saucepan. Bring to a boil over medium-high heat. Cover, reduce heat, and simmer for 25 minutes, or until lentils are tender (you need them to be soft, not mushy!). Remove from the heat, remove the lid, and stir. Set aside to cool completely. Drain.

3. Heat 2 tablespoons of the oil in a skillet over medium-high heat. Add onion and cook, stirring frequently, for 5 minutes. Add garlic, carrot, and curry spice blend and cook, stirring constantly, for 1 minute. Stir in ¼ cup of the remaining broth and bring to a boil. Reduce heat and simmer, stirring frequently, for 10 minutes, or until vegetables are tender, adding more broth if the mixture is too dry.

4. Use a vegetable masher or food processor (a blender will become gummed up) to purée the cooked lentils with the remaining tablespoon of oil. Scrape into a large bowl and add the cooked onion mixture, walnuts, and salt. Add 1 or both tablespoons mustard and mix well to form a soft, moist mixture. (This part is a bit tricky: the mixture has to be soft and moist enough to form patties and not too dry or it will split and break, yet not too wet or it won't hold together.)

5. Divide the mixture into six portions (eight if making sliders) and press between the palms of your hands into round patties (about ¾ inch thick). Arrange on prepared baking sheet and bake for 15 minutes. Remove from oven, cover with foil, and set aside for 10 minutes to firm up.

YOU'VE GOT OPTIONS

You can buy cooked lentils in a can and they will work fine, but look, cooking lentils is not a big deal. If you do use canned, promise me that you'll use those leftover lentils in a burrito or a wrap!

CURRY SPICE BLEND

MAKES ½ CUP

3 tablespoons ground turmeric

2 tablespoons ground fenugreek (see tip)

1 tablespoon ground coriander

1 tablespoon ground cumin

2 teaspoons ground ginger

1 teaspoon ground cayenne pepper (optional)

1 teaspoon ground cinnamon

Combine turmeric, fenugreek, coriander, cumin, ginger, cayenne pepper (if using), and cinnamon in a small bowl. Thoroughly blend using a fork or whisk. Place in a dark-colored jar with tight-fitting lid and store in a cool cupboard.

PAT'S TIP: Fenugreek is the spice that gives curry that unmistakable aroma and flavor. If you can't find fenugreek, just buy a good curry blend instead of trying to make it.

SUMMER SALAD RICE ROLLS

MAKES 10 ROLLS

1 avocado

2 tablespoons freshly squeezed lemon juice

10 (8-inch) round rice paper wrappers

2 stalks celery, cut lengthwise into ¼-inch-wide strips

1 medium carrot, shredded

1 cucumber or zucchini, halved lengthwise and cut into ¼-inch-wide slices

½ red bell pepper, cut lengthwise into ¼-inch-wide strips

½ cup thinly sliced red cabbage or baby spinach

1 handful fresh sprouts

2 ounces cooked rice vermicelli (optional)

⅔ cup shelled raw sunflower seeds

Sea salt (optional)

FOR SERVING (OPTIONAL)

1 cup Peanut Sauce (page 29), or store-bought

TO SERVE

Serve at room temperature with peanut sauce.

1. Cut the avocado in half lengthwise and remove the pit, then peel and cut each half into eight thin slices directly into a bowl. Sprinkle lemon juice over the avocado and lightly toss to coat.

2. Fill a 10-inch pie plate halfway full with warm water. Slide a rice paper wrapper into the water and let it sit for 15 to 20 seconds, until soft and pliable. (It will turn clear when ready. It may take a couple of attempts to figure out the perfect timing.) Remove and lay flat on a work surface. Lay two sticks of celery, a pinch of shredded carrot, two sticks of cucumber, and a piece of red bell pepper in the center. Spread some cabbage, one avocado slice, a pinch of sprouts, and a couple of noodles (if using) over the other vegetables. Sprinkle 1 tablespoon sunflower seeds over the filling and a pinch of salt if desired.

3. Fold each end of the rice paper wrapper (top and bottom) over the filling. Then fold the right side over the filling and spin the paper one-quarter turn to the right. Using two hands, gently pull the covered filling toward you to make a tight roll. Roll the filled half away from you and over the other half of the wrapper. Moisten to seal the edge. Place on a platter, seam side down, and cover with a moistened tea towel.

4. Repeat steps 2 and 3 until all rice paper wrappers have been filled and rolled.

PAT'S TIP: Like most things in life, rolling rice paper gets easier after you make a few wraps. One essential: have all the ingredients peeled and sliced before you start to prepare and roll the wrappers. You'll moisten, fill, and roll one wrapper at a time—so have a platter and a moistened tea towel handy to cover the ones you've finished as you roll the rest. Kids can learn how to roll these (and they don't care if each roll isn't perfect).

TUSCAN PIZZA

MAKES 1 (10-INCH) PIZZA

2 tablespoons extra-virgin olive oil

1 medium onion, thinly sliced

½ red bell pepper, cut into long, thin strips

3 cloves garlic, chopped

1 small zucchini, peeled and thinly sliced

1 (10-inch) uncooked, prerolled pizza crust, thawed if frozen

1 cup Basil Pesto (page 85), or store-bought

1 tomato, cored and sliced

Sea salt (optional)

¼ cup Vegan Parmesan Cheese, Try it! recipe (page 39) or store-bought

GARNISH (OPTIONAL)

¼ to ½ cup fresh basil

1. Preheat oven to 425°F.

2. Heat oil in a skillet over medium-high heat. Add onion and pepper and cook, stirring frequently, for 5 minutes. Add garlic and zucchini and cook, stirring occasionally, for 10 minutes, or until vegetables are tender and fragrant.

3. Meanwhile, place crust on a baking sheet and spread evenly with pesto. Spread sautéed vegetables over pesto and arrange tomato slices on top. Sprinkle a pinch of salt over (if using) and top evenly with vegan Parmesan cheese. Add basil leaves if desired.

4. Bake for 17 to 20 minutes, until crust is lightly browned and topping is bubbling.

Try it!
VEGAN PARMESAN CHEESE

MAKES 1¼ CUPS

1 cup roasted and salted cashews

¼ cup nutritional yeast

½ teaspoon ground turmeric

Combine cashews, yeast, and turmeric in the bowl of a food processor. Process for 1 minute, or until the mixture is finely chopped.

TO STORE
Transfer to a 2-cup-capacity jar with a lid and keep refrigerated for 3 to 4 weeks.

VEGAN CHEESY QUESO

MAKES 1½ CUPS

⅔ cup raw cashews

1 clove garlic

3 tablespoons tapioca flour (see page 14)

1 tablespoon nutritional yeast

1 teaspoon apple cider vinegar

1 teaspoon ground turmeric

½ teaspoon ground cumin

½ teaspoon sea salt

1. Place cashews in a saucepan and cover with 2 cups water or to cover. Bring to a boil over medium-high heat and boil for 15 minutes, or until soft. Drain over a liquid measuring cup to reserve the cooking liquid.

2. Combine 1 cup of the reserved cooking water with the cashews, garlic, tapioca flour, nutritional yeast, vinegar, turmeric, cumin, and salt in the jug of a blender. Process for 30 to 60 seconds, until smooth.

3. Pour mixture into the same saucepan used to boil the cashews and cook over medium-high heat, stirring constantly, for 3 to 5 minutes, until the mixture is firmed up. (You need to keep stirring to move the thickened mixture at the bottom of the pan so that the liquid on top can reach the heat and become thickened.) The mixture will be soft yet firm and stretchy, like melted mozzarella cheese.)

YOU'VE GOT OPTIONS

Add some heat with ½ to 1 teaspoon red pepper flakes in step 2.

TO SERVE

Queso is best served warm, so if you have a small slow cooker, a flameproof bowl and tea light warmer, or a warming tray, any of these would be ideal for serving. Use as a dip for nachos, crackers, vegetables, or fruit.

Try combining the queso with 2 cups chopped spinach and 1 cup drained, chopped, marinated, canned artichoke hearts for an easy dip.

TO STORE

Best if made and used immediately but can be covered and refrigerated for up to 2 days. Reheat before serving.

TOASTED SPICED WALNUTS

MAKES 3 CUPS

SEE PHOTOGRAPH ON PAGE 6

1 tablespoon coconut sugar

1 tablespoon Garam Masala Spice Blend
(page 25), or store-bought

1 teaspoon kosher salt or coarsely ground
sea salt

½ teaspoon ground allspice

3 cups shelled whole walnuts (see options)

2 tablespoons extra-virgin avocado oil

1. Preheat oven to 375°F. Line a rimmed baking sheet with parchment paper.

2. Combine coconut sugar, spice blend, salt, and allspice in a small bowl and set aside.

3. Arrange walnuts in one layer on the prepared baking sheet. Drizzle oil over them and toss to coat. Sprinkle seasoning mixture over them and again spread the nuts out in one layer on the baking sheet.

4. Bake for 4 minutes. Stir and spread out in one layer, return to oven, and bake for 3 minutes, or until lightly browned.

TO STORE

Spiced walnuts keep in an airtight container at room temperature for up to 5 days or in the refrigerator for up to 2 weeks.

YOU'VE GOT OPTIONS

Any nut—almonds, pecans, cashews, pistachios, *any* nut—will work in this recipe.

½ cup unflavored, unsweetened organic soy milk, room temperature (see tips)

2 teaspoons apple cider vinegar, room temperature

1 teaspoon Dijon mustard, room temperature

½ teaspoon sea salt

¾ to 1 cup sunflower oil, room temperature

1. Combine soy milk, vinegar, mustard, and salt in the blender jug. Put the lid on and blend on high for 2 seconds.

2. With the motor running on medium-high or blend, slowly add the oil through the opening in the lid. Blend for about 2 minutes, or until the mixture thickens. (You may not need all of the oil. The more oil you add, the thicker the mayonnaise will be.)

PAT'S TIPS: First, this will only work with soy milk. Second, all of the ingredients must be at room temperature for the protein in the soy to emulsify the oil.

TO STORE

Use immediately or transfer leftovers to a 1-cup-capacity jar, cap, and store in the refrigerator for up to 5 days.

AVOCADO DIP

MAKES 1 CUP, EASILY DOUBLED

2 tablespoons freshly squeezed lemon
juice

2 ripe avocados

3 tablespoons Vegan Mayonnaise, Try it!
recipe (page 43) or store-bought

1 to 2 cloves garlic, minced (see options)

1 to 2 teaspoons sriracha sauce or hot
sauce (optional)

Sea salt

GARNISH (OPTIONAL)

2 tablespoons finely chopped fresh
cilantro or oregano

TO SERVE
Scrape into a serving bowl and
garnish with cilantro if desired.

TO USE
Avocado dip is a great
substitute for mayonnaise in
wraps, burritos, and sandwiches,
and it makes a great topping for
any of the dinner bowls or main
courses in this book. Having this
dip or guacamole on hand is like
having fresh avocado slices at
your disposal.

TO STORE
Avocado dip keeps in a
covered container in the
refrigerator for up to 1 week.

1. Pour lemon juice into a medium-sized bowl. Cut 1 avocado
   in half and remove the pit, then peel and slice each half
   directly over the bowl, letting the pieces fall into the
   lemon juice. Toss gently to coat with lemon juice. Repeat
   with remaining avocado.

2. Mash the avocado and lemon juice together roughly
   with a fork or potato masher. Add mayonnaise, garlic, and
   sriracha sauce (if using) and stir well to mix. Taste and add
   salt to taste.

YOU'VE GOT OPTIONS

- I think avocado dip should be garlicky, but you can swap
  a couple of tablespoons of finely chopped chives for the
  garlic if you like a milder version. (Use 2 tablespoons
  chopped chives, taste and add more as desired.)

- Try adding a fresh tomato, cored, seeded, and chopped.

AVOCADO FRIES

MAKES 8 FRIES, EASILY DOUBLED OR TRIPLED

1 tablespoon flaxseeds or chia seeds

1 cup bread crumbs

¼ cup all-purpose or chickpea flour

Juice of ½ lemon

1 large avocado

Kosher salt or coarsely ground sea salt

FOR SERVING (OPTIONAL)

1 cup Chipotle Dipping Sauce, Try it! recipe (page 48) or store-bought

1. Preheat oven to 400°F.

2. Combine 2 tablespoons water and flaxseeds in a small bowl. Set aside for 10 minutes.

3. Meanwhile, prepare ingredients for coating the avocado: Spread bread crumbs in a shallow dish. Spread flour in a separate shallow dish.

4. Pour lemon juice into a medium-sized bowl. Cut avocado in half and remove the pit, then peel and slice each half into four thick wedges, letting the wedges fall into the lemon juice. Toss gently to coat with lemon juice.

5. Working one piece at a time, dredge an avocado wedge in flour, then coat with flaxseed mixture, and then dredge in bread crumbs. Place on a baking sheet. Coat remaining avocado wedges.

6. Bake for 10 minutes. Using tongs, turn wedges over and bake for 20 minutes more, or until coating is brown. Sprinkle with salt. Serve with the dipping sauce on the side.

Try it!
CHIPOTLE DIPPING SAUCE

MAKES 1 CUP

1 large or 2 small canned chipotle chile(s) in adobo sauce (see options)

1 tablespoon adobo sauce (see options)

1 green onion, thinly sliced, or 2 tablespoons chopped onion

1 cup Vegan Mayonnaise (page 43), or store-bought

Combine chile(s), sauce, and green onions in the bowl of a food processor. Process for 30 seconds, or until chopped. Add mayonnaise and process for about 30 seconds, or until ingredients are blended and smooth.

TO STORE

Transfer to a 1-cup-capacity jar with a lid. It will keep in the refrigerator for up to 2 weeks.

TO USE

As a dipping sauce: Serve with raw or cooked vegetables; drizzle over tacos, burritos, or wraps; or offer with Baked Onion Rings (page 24). As a dressing: Thin the sauce with 1 tablespoon freshly squeezed lemon juice to make it the consistency of vinaigrette, for tossing with salads.

YOU'VE GOT OPTIONS

- Each brand of chiles in adobo sauce is different: some have a lot of sauce, some not so much. If the can or jar that you have doesn't have enough sauce to use in this recipe, you can use prepared barbecue sauce (ketchup will also work) in place of the adobo sauce.

- If you really love the smoky heat of chipotle chiles, go ahead and use 2 or even 3 large ones in this recipe.

COCOA ENERGY BARS

MAKES 16 (2-INCH) BARS

SEE PHOTOGRAPH ON PAGE VI

¾ cup unsweetened shredded coconut

½ cup rolled oats

½ cup shelled raw sunflower seeds or hemp seeds

⅓ cup carob or cocoa powder

½ teaspoon ground cinnamon

1½ cups coarsely chopped dates

1 teaspoon pure vanilla extract

1 teaspoon sea salt

¾ cup Chocolate Icing (page 207), or store-bought (optional)

TO STORE

Bars will keep in the refrigerator for up to a week. Store in a parchment-lined tin or plastic container with tight-fitting lid.

1. Lightly oil the sides of an 8 by 8 by 2-inch baking pan and line the bottom with parchment paper.

2. Combine coconut, oats, seeds, carob powder, and cinnamon in the bowl of a food processor. Process for about 30 seconds, or until ingredients are finely chopped. Add dates, vanilla, and salt. Process for 1 minute, or until mixture begins to stick together and starts to form a ball. Add a tablespoon of warm water if necessary to make the mixture stick together.

3. Transfer to the prepared pan and press evenly with the back of a wooden spoon. Cover with plastic wrap and chill for at least 30 minutes.

4. If using, spread icing evenly over and cut into 2-inch squares.

FAST AND EASY FALAFEL

MAKES ABOUT 24 SMALL FALAFEL

1 teaspoon sea salt, divided

½ cup quinoa

2 green onions, chopped

2 large cloves garlic

¼ cup chopped fresh cilantro or parsley

1 (16-ounce) can chickpeas, drained and rinsed

1 teaspoon ground cumin

3 tablespoons freshly squeezed lemon juice

½ cup chickpea or all-purpose flour, plus more if needed

4 tablespoons extra-virgin avocado oil, plus more as needed

FOR SERVING (OPTIONAL)

1 cup Cucumber Relish, Try it! recipe (page 52)

1 cup Peanut Sauce (page 29), or store-bought

1 cup Chipotle Dipping Sauce (page 48), or store-bought

1. Line a large platter with paper towels or a tea towel.

2. Bring 1 cup water and ½ teaspoon of the salt to a boil in a saucepan over high heat. Stir in quinoa and bring back to a boil. Cover, reduce heat, and simmer for 15 to 20 minutes, until the water is absorbed and the grain is tender, light, and fluffy. Stir, remove from heat, and set aside to cool completely.

3. Combine green onions, garlic, and cilantro in the bowl of a food processor. Process for 30 seconds, or until chopped. Add chickpeas, cumin, remaining ½ teaspoon of salt, cooked quinoa, and lemon juice. Process until smooth. Test consistency and add flour by the tablespoon until the mixture holds together for cooking.

4. Spread flour in a shallow dish and lightly dust your palms with some. Scoop 1 or 2 tablespoons of the mixture into your hands and roll it into a ball, dusting it with flour after it is rolled. Set on a plate or baking sheet. Repeat until all of the mixture has been formed into balls. You should have about 24 balls.

5. Heat 2 tablespoons of oil in a skillet over medium-high heat. Using a spoon, add 3 or 4 balls to the pan and fry, turning often with a fork, for about 4 minutes, or until golden brown all over. Lift out and place on the platter.

6. Continue cooking remaining balls in batches, adding more oil to the skillet as needed.

TO SERVE

Serve as an appetizer or snack with Cucumber Relish (page 52), Peanut Sauce (page 29), or Chipotle Dipping Sauce (page 48).

TO USE

Cooked falafel can be tossed with salads, added to Tomato Sauce (page 146), or stuffed into pita pockets or taco shells along with lettuce, tomato, and onions.

Try it!
CUCUMBER RELISH

MAKES 3 CUPS, EASILY HALVED

½ cup apple cider vinegar

½ cup granulated sugar

1 tablespoon Garam Masala Spice Blend
(page 25), or store-bought

1 tablespoon Dijon mustard

½ teaspoon sea salt

1 cucumber, peel on, cut into small dice
(about 2 cups)

½ red bell pepper, finely chopped

½ medium onion, finely chopped

1. Combine vinegar, sugar, spice blend, mustard, and salt in a nonreactive saucepan. Bring to a boil over medium-high heat. Reduce heat to medium-low and simmer, stirring occasionally, for 5 minutes, or until slightly thickened. Remove from heat and set aside to cool completely.

2. Combine cucumber, pepper, and onion in a bowl. Drizzle vinegar mixture over the vegetables and toss to coat.

TO USE

Lift relish out of the bowl or jar using a slotted spoon or fork to drain off the excess vinegar. Use as a condiment for Black Bean Burgers (page 176) or Lentil Sliders (page 34), or as a relish/salsa for wraps, tacos, or burritos. Serve with Grilled Skewered Eggplant (page 28), or add to any of the "Dinner in a Bowl" meals (starting on page 83).

TO STORE

Transfer relish and vinegar mixture to a 4-cup-capacity jar with a lid. Store in the refrigerator for up to 4 weeks.

ROASTED RED PEPPER HUMMUS

MAKES ABOUT 3 CUPS

SEE PHOTOGRAPH ON PAGE 20

1 (16-ounce) can chickpeas

¼ cup shelled raw sunflower seeds

3 cloves garlic

2 tablespoons freshly squeezed lemon juice

2 tablespoons tahini

1 roasted red bell pepper, drained if canned

½ teaspoon sea salt

1. Drain chickpeas over a bowl to reserve the liquid. Rinse chickpeas and set them and the reserved liquid aside.

2. Combine sunflower seeds and garlic in the bowl of a food processor. Process for 30 seconds, or until chopped. Add lemon juice, tahini, pepper, salt, and drained chickpeas. Process for 30 seconds. Scrape down the sides of the bowl and add reserved chickpea liquid, 1 tablespoon at a time, through the opening in the funnel and process until mixture is smooth. The more liquid you add, the thinner the mixture will be.

TO STORE

The hummus keeps in a covered container in the refrigerator for up to 1 week.

YOU'VE GOT OPTIONS

I find that a blender is not the best tool to use for this recipe, but if you don't have a food processor, you can still make it. Here's how: Omit the sunflower seeds; mince the garlic and finely chop the pepper. After step 1, place the chickpeas in a bowl and mash using a potato masher. Add the garlic, lemon juice, tahini, pepper, and salt and mix well. Add reserved chickpea liquid, 1 tablespoon at a time, and stir until a thick, smooth consistency is achieved.

SPICED SRIRACHA POPCORN

MAKES 10 CUPS

3 tablespoons extra-virgin avocado oil, divided

½ cup popcorn kernels (see options)

⅓ cup coconut nectar (see options)

1 teaspoon ground cinnamon (see options)

½ to 1 teaspoon sriracha sauce

½ teaspoon coarse salt or to taste

1. Heat 2 tablespoons of the oil over high heat in a large pot with a lid. Add kernels and shake the pot to coat them with oil. Cover. As soon as the kernels start to pop, reduce heat to medium-low and cook, shaking the pot once, for 6 minutes, or until popcorn has finished popping. Transfer to a large bowl.

2. Make the sauce: Heat remaining tablespoon of oil, nectar, cinnamon, and sriracha in a saucepan over medium-high heat. Bring to a boil, stirring constantly. Drizzle over popcorn and toss using 2 large spoons. Add salt to taste.

YOU'VE GOT OPTIONS

- This recipe calls for you to pop your own kernels because it's more economical than microwave or prepopped popcorn and you are in control of the ingredients. However, for real convenience, you can use 10 cups of prepopped popcorn (one large bag) and follow step 2 as written, using 1 tablespoon of oil.

- Coconut nectar is a dark brown, tartly sweet syrup with malt and molasses overtones. You can substitute maple syrup or rice syrup.

- If you prefer, instead of cinnamon, use store-bought or your own Garam Masala Spice Blend (page 25) or Curry Spice Blend (page 35).

SPINACH AND ARTICHOKE DIP

MAKES 6 CUPS, EASILY HALVED

3 cups frozen chopped spinach, thawed (see options)

1½ cups Vegan Cheesy Queso (page 41)

1 to 1½ cups unflavored, unsweetened nondairy milk

1 (24-ounce) jar marinated artichoke hearts, drained, roughly chopped, and rinsed

1 small onion, chopped

1 clove garlic, finely chopped, plus more if desired (see options)

½ teaspoon sea salt

¼ cup Vegan Parmesan Cheese (page 39), or store-bought (optional)

FOR SERVING (OPTIONAL)

1 baguette French bread, sliced

Crackers

Tortilla chips

1. Preheat oven to 400°F.

2. Lightly squeeze the spinach to remove excess liquid. Combine spinach, queso, milk, artichokes, onion, garlic, and salt together in a bowl. Use a slotted spoon to mix the ingredients. Scrape into a heatproof casserole dish. Sprinkle vegan Parmesan cheese over the top (if using).

3. Bake for 10 minutes, or until slightly brown and bubbly.

YOU'VE GOT OPTIONS

- Frozen spinach and kale are convenient and either works well in this recipe.

- This dip is mildly garlicky, so add more garlic to suit your taste.

TO SERVE

The dip is best served warm, so if you have a small slow cooker, a flameproof bowl and tea light warmer, or a warming tray, any of these would be ideal for serving. Use as a dip for nachos, tortilla chips, crackers, vegetables, or fruit.

TO STORE

Best if used immediately. Dispose of leftover dip.

Almond Banana Muffins, page 60

BREAKFAST
FAVORITES

ALMOND BANANA MUFFINS

MAKES 1 DOZEN MUFFINS

SEE PHOTOGRAPH ON PAGE 58

1 tablespoon ground flaxseeds or chia seeds

1¾ cup all-purpose flour or gluten-free flour blend

1½ teaspoons baking powder

¾ teaspoon ground cinnamon

½ teaspoon sea salt

¼ teaspoon ground allspice

1 ripe banana

1 cup unflavored, unsweetened or vanilla almond milk

⅓ cup Almond Butter, Try it! recipe (page 61) or store-bought

½ cup coconut sugar

3 tablespoons extra-virgin olive oil

1 teaspoon pure vanilla extract

FOR SERVING (OPTIONAL)

Almond Butter, Try it! recipe (page 61) or store-bought

1. Preheat oven to 375°F. Line a 12-well muffin pan with paper cups or lightly oil.

2. Combine flaxseeds and 3 tablespoons water in a large mixing bowl. Set aside for about 10 minutes.

3. Meanwhile, combine flour, baking powder, cinnamon, salt, and allspice in a separate large bowl. Whisk to mix well.

4. Slice banana into the flaxseed mixture and mash using a fork. Add milk and whisk to combine. Add almond butter and whisk to combine. Add sugar, oil, and vanilla and whisk to combine. Add the flour mixture and stir to mix well. (Stir just until blended; don't overmix or the muffins will rise to a point when baked.)

5. Spoon batter into prepared muffin pan, filling the wells about three-quarters full. Bake for 14 to 20 minutes, until a toothpick inserted into the middle of a muffin comes out clean.

TO SERVE
Cool in the pan for 5 minutes and serve warm with almond butter.

TO STORE
Keep muffins in an airtight container at room temperature for up to 3 days and in the refrigerator for up to 1 week.

Try it! ALMOND BUTTER

MAKES 1¼ CUPS

2 cups roasted or raw almonds (see options)

¼ cup extra-virgin olive oil, divided

¼ teaspoon sea salt

1 tablespoon coconut sugar (optional)

PAT'S TIP: Making almond butter is easy but takes a little patience. The key here, as explained in step 1, is to add a tablespoon of oil, process, and scrape down the bowl (you have to get underneath the blades, too) before adding the next tablespoon of oil.

1. Combine almonds, 1 tablespoon of the oil, salt, and sugar (if using) in the bowl of a food processor. Process for 1 minute. Stop and scrape down the sides of the bowl and add 1 tablespoon of the oil. Process for 1 minute.

2. Keep scraping the bowl and adding 1 tablespoon of the oil until all of the oil has been used and the mixture reaches the consistency of smooth, thick butter. You can thin it by adding 1 tablespoon warm water and processing until combined.

TO STORE

Transfer the nut butter to a 2-cup-capacity jar with a lid and keep in the refrigerator for up to 2 weeks. Bring to room temperature before using. If the oil rises to the top, stir before using.

YOU'VE GOT OPTIONS

- No almonds? No worries—use *any* nuts in this recipe (or sunflower or pumpkin seeds). I prefer to use roasted and salted nuts or seeds because the flavor is more intense, but raw nuts work just as well. You may not need to add as much oil to the butter if using softer nuts, such as walnuts, cashews, or pine nuts.

- Add 1 teaspoon ground cinnamon or ground ginger to punch up the flavor of any nut or seed butter.

APPLE WALNUT PANCAKES

MAKES 8 LARGE PANCAKES

1½ cups all-purpose or gluten-free flour blend

1 tablespoon coconut sugar

2 teaspoons baking powder

¼ teaspoon sea salt

½ cup finely chopped walnuts

1 small apple, finely chopped

1½ cups unsweetened almond or rice milk

½ cup applesauce

2 tablespoons melted extra-virgin olive oil

1 teaspoon pure vanilla extract (optional)

1. Lightly oil a heavy-bottomed skillet or griddle.

2. Combine flour, sugar, baking powder, and salt in a batter bowl or mixing bowl. Whisk with a fork to mix well. Add walnuts and apples and toss to coat.

3. Combine milk, applesauce, oil, and vanilla (if using) in a 2-cup measuring cup. Whisk with a fork until smooth. Make a well in the center of the flour mixture. Scrape liquid ingredients into flour mixture and gently mix just until combined (the batter may have small lumps; that's okay).

4. Heat oiled skillet over medium-high heat. Ladle about ½ cup batter (for large pancakes) into the skillet and flatten to about ¼ inch thick using the back of a spoon. Ladle in as many pancakes as will fit in the pan without running together. Cook for about 2 minutes, or until brown on the underside with small bubbles on the top. Flip and cook on opposite side for 1 minute, or until brown. Serve while hot or keep warm on a baking sheet in a 300°F oven.

5. Repeat step 4 until all of the batter has been cooked.

YOU'VE GOT OPTIONS

- Substitute ¾ cup blueberries (thawed if frozen) for the apple and/or walnuts.

- Spice it up! Add ½ teaspoon ground cinnamon or chili powder to dry ingredients in step 2.

RASPBERRY COOKIE SMOOTHIE BOWL

MAKES 1 SERVING, EASILY DOUBLED

SEE PHOTOGRAPH ON PAGE XII

¾ cup unflavored, unsweetened or vanilla nondairy milk (see options)

1 cup frozen raspberries (see options)

¼ cup High-Energy Granola (page 70), or store-bought (see options)

1 tablespoon Almond Butter (page 61), or store-bought, or cashew butter (see options)

GARNISH (OPTIONAL)

¼ cup fresh or thawed frozen raspberries

2 tablespoons High-Energy Granola (page 70), or store-bought

2 tablespoons shredded coconut (sweetened or unsweetened)

1. Combine milk, raspberries, granola, and almond butter in the jug of a blender. Blend for 20 seconds, or until smooth. Pour into a cereal bowl.

2. If desired, garnish with whole raspberries and sprinkle granola and coconut over the top.

   PAT'S TIP: Using frozen berries in this recipe results in a spoonable breakfast that can also be served as a drink.

YOU'VE GOT OPTIONS

- If you don't have granola, use rolled oats (instant or regular) in its place.

- Any nut butter will work in this recipe.

- Frozen berries—you can use any berry here—make the mixture thick, but if you use fresh berries, reduce the amount of milk to about ¼ cup.

BERRY SMOOTHIE

MAKES 1 SERVING, EASILY DOUBLED

¾ cup unflavored, unsweetened or vanilla nondairy milk

1 cup frozen mixed berries (see options)

¼ cup Vegan Yogurt, Try it! recipe (page 66) or store-bought (optional)

1 tablespoon nut butter (any kind)

2 teaspoons chia seeds (optional)

Combine milk, berries, yogurt (if using), nut butter, and chia seeds (if using) in the jug of a blender. Blend on high for 1 minute, or until smooth.

YOU'VE GOT OPTIONS

- Keep a bag of frozen berries—strawberries, blackberries, raspberries, blueberries, acai berries, or a mix of these—to pop into the blender for thick, tangy smoothies with antioxidant properties.

- If you have fresh berries on hand, use them! Reduce the amount of milk by at least half to keep the smoothie thick.

- If you have Almond Butter (page 61), use it here.

BE SMOOTHIE SAVVY

Smoothies are the perfect vehicle for delivering health benefits from herbs, fruit, vegetables, grains, and nuts. Keep on hand hemp seeds, pumpkin seeds, chia seeds, and flaxseeds, and matcha, plant-based protein powder, and antioxidant herbs (thyme, sage, rosemary), as well as medicinal herbs (turmeric, elderberry, echinacea, astragalus), to add to the blender (not all in the same smoothie).

Try it! VEGAN YOGURT

MAKES 1¾ CUPS

1 cup raw cashews

3 tablespoons freshly squeezed lemon juice

1 tablespoon soft extra-virgin coconut oil

1 teaspoon nutritional yeast

¼ teaspoon sea salt

TO STORE

Transfer to a 2-cup-capacity jar with a lid. Yogurt keeps in the refrigerator for up to 1 week.

1. Place cashews in a bowl or large liquid measuring cup. Add cool water to cover, so that they are floating. Cover and set aside at room temperature for 4 hours or in the refrigerator overnight.

2. **Four Hours Later (or the Next Day):** Drain cashews, reserving ½ cup of the liquid.

3. Combine cashews, lemon juice, oil, yeast, and salt in the bowl of a small food processor. Process on high for 10 seconds, until mixed. With the motor running, slowly add the reserved liquid through the opening in the lid until the mixture is thick and creamy. (You may have to stop and scrape down the sides of the bowl once or twice.)

CHOCOLATE CHIA SMOOTHIE

MAKES 1 SERVING, EASILY DOUBLED

½ cup canned coconut milk

1 tablespoon chia seeds

½ ripe banana

6 raw almonds

1 tablespoon cocoa or carob powder

1. Combine milk and chia seeds in the jug of a blender. Blend for 10 seconds and let stand for 5 minutes.

2. Add banana, almonds, and cocoa powder. Blend for 30 seconds, or until smooth.

GREEN SMOOTHIE BOWL WITH GRANOLA

MAKES 1 SERVING, EASILY DOUBLED

3 tablespoons unflavored, unsweetened or vanilla nondairy milk

¾ cup applesauce or crushed pineapple

1 cup fresh or frozen baby spinach

1 ripe banana, cut into 3 or 4 chunks

1 teaspoon matcha (optional)

1 teaspoon softened extra-virgin coconut oil

2 tablespoons High-Energy Granola, Try it! recipe (page 70) or store-bought

1. Combine milk, applesauce, spinach, banana, matcha (if using), and oil in the jug of a blender. Blend on high for 30 seconds to 1 minute, until smooth.

2. Pour into a cereal bowl and top with granola.

PAT'S TIP: One cup of fresh greens can be roughly measured as a woman's handful or a man's slight handful.

YOU'VE GOT OPTIONS

- Try adding instant oatmeal to the smoothie after pouring into the bowl.

- Top with Vegan Yogurt (page 66), nuts, or dried fruit.

Try it!
HIGH-ENERGY GRANOLA

MAKES 4 TO 6 SERVINGS

1½ cups rolled oats

⅔ cup coarsely chopped pecans

⅔ cup coarsely chopped walnuts

⅓ cup shelled raw sunflower seeds

¼ teaspoon sea salt

¼ cup coconut nectar or pure maple syrup

¼ cup extra-virgin coconut oil

1½ teaspoons ground cinnamon

1. Preheat oven to 300°F. Line a rimmed baking sheet with parchment paper.

2. Combine oats, pecans, walnuts, sunflower seeds, and salt together in a large bowl.

3. Combine nectar, oil, and cinnamon together in a saucepan. Bring to a simmer over medium-high heat. Drizzle over oat mixture and toss to mix well. Spread out on the prepared baking sheet.

4. Bake for 35 minutes, or until dry and browned. Set aside to cool completely.

TO STORE
Break the cooled granola into small pieces and store in a parchment-lined tin or plastic container with a tight-fitting lid. Granola will keep in a cool cupboard for up to 1 month.

FRENCH TOAST

MAKES 2 TO 3 SERVINGS

2 tablespoons ground flaxseeds or chia seeds

1 tablespoon coconut sugar (optional)

½ teaspoon ground cinnamon

1 cup unflavored, unsweetened or vanilla nondairy milk

½ teaspoon pure vanilla extract

1 tablespoon extra-virgin avocado oil

4 slices whole wheat bread (see tip)

FOR TOPPING (OPTIONAL)

¼ cup Vegan Yogurt (page 66), or store-bought

¼ cup Almond Butter (page 61), or store-bought

1. Combine flaxseeds, sugar (if using), and cinnamon in a mixing bowl and stir well. Place milk in a liquid measuring cup and whisk in vanilla using a fork. Whisk milk mixture into flaxseed mixture until well mixed. Set aside for about 12 minutes. Stir to mix.

2. Heat oil in a griddle or heavy-bottomed skillet over medium-high heat.

3. Dip a slice of bread in the milk batter so that it absorbs some of the batter. (Don't leave it in the batter too long or it will get soggy.) Lift out and cook in hot skillet for 1 to 2 minutes, until golden brown on the underside. Flip over and cook for 1 to 2 minutes, until golden brown.

4. Repeat step 3 with remaining slices of bread. If desired, top each slice of French toast with 1 tablespoon each of vegan yogurt and almond butter.

PAT'S TIP: Use a firm, country-style bread that won't break down and get soggy in the milk mixture. (Day-old bread also works.)

CHERRY PECAN OATMEAL

MAKES 2 TO 3 SERVINGS

2 cups unflavored, unsweetened or vanilla nondairy milk

1 cup rolled oats (see options)

⅓ cup coarsely chopped pecans (see options)

¼ cup dried cherries (see options)

½ teaspoon ground cinnamon

¼ teaspoon sea salt

Pure maple syrup, for serving

1. Bring milk to a boil in a saucepan over medium-high heat. Stir in oats and bring back to a simmer. Adjust heat to around medium-low to keep mixture simmering.

2. Stir in pecans, cherries, cinnamon, and salt. Stir to mix well. Cook, stirring frequently, for 5 to 7 minutes, until the milk has been absorbed. Stir more frequently toward the end of the cooking time to keep the mixture from sticking to the pan.

3. Divide oatmeal into two or three cereal bowls. Serve with maple syrup.

YOU'VE GOT OPTIONS

- Rolled oats are used in this recipe; however, steel-cut oats are delicious, and they are more nutrient-rich than rolled oats because they have not been processed (rolled and steamed). If you are gluten sensitive, be sure to buy a brand that guarantees that the oats were not grown where wheat grows and that they were processed in a wheat-free plant.

- Try quinoa, amaranth, spelt flakes, or brown rice in this classic breakfast dish. The amount of milk and grain and the method remain the same, but the cooking time may be longer for quinoa, and about 35 to 40 minutes for brown rice.

- Any nut can be substituted for the pecans in this recipe.

- Change it up and use blueberries, apricot pieces, cranberries, or other dried fruit in place of the cherries.

- Serve with Vegan Yogurt (page 66) or cold almond milk.

BREAKFAST ACAI BOWL

MAKES 1 SERVING, EASILY DOUBLED

½ cup quinoa or rolled oats

½ teaspoon sea salt

¼ cup frozen acai berries or blueberries (see options)

2 tablespoons shredded coconut

2 tablespoons pure maple syrup

½ ripe banana

1 tablespoon dried goji berries or dried cherries

¼ teaspoon ground cinnamon

¼ cup unflavored, unsweetened or vanilla nondairy milk (optional)

¼ cup Vegan Yogurt (page 66), or store-bought (optional)

1. Bring 1 cup water to a boil in a saucepan over medium-high heat. Stir in quinoa and salt. Bring back to a boil, reduce heat, and simmer, stirring often, for 6 minutes, or until grain is cooked. Stir in acai berries and coconut. Scrape into a cereal bowl and drizzle with maple syrup.

2. Slice banana over the top of the quinoa and sprinkle goji berries and cinnamon over it. Add milk (if using). Serve with vegan yogurt, if desired.

YOU'VE GOT OPTIONS

- Try a new grain; check out Amazing Grains, page 8.

- Acai berries are awesome! They taste like chocolate and blueberries—yum! And like blueberries, they are high in antioxidants. Look for them in the frozen fruit section at specialty food stores. Any frozen berry will work in place of acai berries.

- Dried cherries add a tart flavor, but try other dried fruit as well: apricots (chopped), cranberries, blueberries, apples... Keep a selection on hand to add to breakfasts and dinner bowls.

TOFU SCRAMBLE

MAKES 3 TO 4 SERVINGS (2 CUPS), EASILY DOUBLED

8 ounces organic firm tofu

2 tablespoons nutritional yeast

1 tablespoon Curry Spice Blend (page 35),
  or store-bought

1 tablespoon pure maple syrup

1 tablespoon soy sauce or tamari

2 tablespoons extra-virgin avocado oil

1 small onion, finely chopped

½ red bell pepper, thinly sliced

1 clove garlic, minced (optional)

1 cup baby spinach leaves

Sea salt (optional)

FOR SERVING (OPTIONAL)

¼ cup Tomato Salsa, Try it! recipe
  (page 78) or store-bought (see options)

1. Squeeze tofu over the sink using your hands. Roughly chop and set aside in a colander to drain.

2. Combine yeast, spice blend, maple syrup, and soy sauce with 2 tablespoons hot water in a medium-sized bowl. Add chopped tofu and break up with a potato masher or fork, mixing evenly with the yeast mixture. Set aside.

3. Melt oil in a skillet over medium heat. Add onion, pepper, and garlic (if using) and cook, stirring frequently, for 6 minutes, or until onion is soft and fragrant. Stir in tofu and cook, stirring occasionally, for about 8 minutes, or until tofu is warmed through. Add spinach and cook, stirring constantly, for 1 minute, or until wilted.

4. Taste and add salt if required. Serve with tomato salsa if desired.

YOU'VE GOT OPTIONS

- If you have Cucumber Relish (page 52) or Basil Pesto (page 85), use either in place of the tomato salsa.

- For a hearty breakfast, roast potatoes and serve with the scramble.

- Make enough so that you can have Breakfast Burritos (page 80) the next day.

Try it!
TOMATO SALSA

MAKES 2 CUPS

1 (28-ounce) can diced tomatoes

2 tablespoons balsamic vinegar

1 tablespoon coconut sugar

1 teaspoon adobo sauce (optional)

2 green onions, thinly sliced, or
   2 tablespoons finely chopped onion

1 clove garlic, minced

1 canned chipotle pepper, finely chopped

½ cup chopped fresh cilantro (optional)

¼ teaspoon sea salt or more to taste

1. Place tomatoes in a fine-mesh strainer set over a 2-cup measuring cup. Set aside to drain for at least 20 minutes. Discard tomato liquids or set aside to use in vegetable broth or another recipe.

2. Combine vinegar, sugar, and adobo sauce (if using) in a bowl. Stir in tomatoes, green onions, garlic, chipotle, and cilantro (if using) and toss to mix well. Taste and add salt if desired.

TO STORE

Tomato salsa keeps in a nonreactive, covered container in the refrigerator for up to 1 week.

TO USE

For pasta: This makes an incredibly easy sauce for pasta, and you can make it in the time it takes to cook the noodles.

For pizza: For a smoother pizza sauce, process the salsa for 30 seconds in the blender.

For bruschetta: Cut French bread into slices ½ inch thick and spread 2 or 3 tablespoons of the salsa over top of each slice; sprinkle with Vegan Parmesan Cheese (page 39) and broil for 30 seconds.

It also makes an excellent sauce for any "Dinner in a Bowl" recipe (see page 83) and a great dipping sauce for wraps, sandwiches, and burritos.

BREAKFAST BURRITOS

MAKES 4 BURRITOS

2 tablespoons extra-virgin avocado oil

1 small onion, chopped

1 cup shredded potato

1½ cups chopped kale

4 (10-inch) soft tortillas

3 tablespoons hummus (see options)

2 cups Tofu Scramble (page 77)

½ cup Tomato Salsa (page 78), or
   store-bought

1. Heat oil in a skillet over medium-high heat. Add onion and potato and cook, stirring frequently, for 5 minutes, or until onion is soft. Add 2 tablespoons water, cover, and cook for 6 minutes, or until potato is fork-tender. Add kale and cook, stirring frequently, for 2 minutes, or until warmed through.

2. Assemble burritos: Work with one tortilla at a time. Spread 1 tablespoon hummus (if using) over one-half of the tortilla. Spoon ½ cup of the tofu scramble over the hummus.

3. Divide potato mixture into four equal portions and spread one portion over tofu scramble. Spoon 2 tablespoons salsa over potatoes. Fold each end of the tortilla (top and bottom) over the filling. Then fold the right side over the filling and spin the tortilla one-quarter turn to the right so that the filling is closest to you. Using two hands, gently pull the covered filling toward you to make a tight roll. Roll the filled half of the tortilla away from you and over the rest of the tortilla. Secure with toothpicks if you like.

YOU'VE GOT OPTIONS

Use Roasted Red Pepper Hummus (page 53), or store-bought, or swap hummus for Vegan Mayonnaise (page 43), Peanut Sauce (page 29), or Chipotle Dipping Sauce (page 48).

Broccoli Pesto Noodle Bowl, page 84

DINNER IN A BOWL

BROCCOLI PESTO NOODLE BOWL

MAKES 4 SERVINGS

SEE PHOTOGRAPH ON PAGE 82

8 ounces soba or udon noodles

½ teaspoon sea salt, plus more to taste

4 cups broccoli florets

1 cup frozen lima beans, green beans, or wax beans

½ cup Basil Pesto, Try it! recipe (page 85) or store-bought

GARNISH (OPTIONAL)

½ cup Roasted Red Pepper Hummus (page 53), or store-bought

½ cup chopped walnuts

1. Bring a large pot of water to a boil over high heat. Add noodles and salt. Bring back to a boil and cook for 6 to 8 minutes, until al dente. Lift noodles from water using tongs, leaving the water in the pot, and transfer to a colander. Rinse and set aside to drain.

2. Add broccoli to the hot noodle water and bring to a boil over high heat. Reduce heat to medium-low and simmer for 4 minutes. Add lima beans, increase heat to high, and bring back to a boil. Cook for 2 minutes, or until broccoli is fork-tender and beans are heated through. Drain.

TO SERVE

Toss noodles and pesto in a large bowl, taste, and add sea salt if desired. Divide evenly among four serving bowls. Spoon broccoli and lima beans over noodles in each bowl. Spoon 2 tablespoons hummus (if using) into the center of the bowls and sprinkle the chopped walnuts (if using) over the top.

Try it! BASIL PESTO

MAKES 2 CUPS

1 cup roasted and salted cashews

¼ cup nutritional yeast

½ teaspoon ground turmeric

3 cloves garlic

⅓ cup pine nuts or shelled raw sunflower seeds

4 packed cups fresh basil

Pinch of sea salt

1 cup extra-virgin olive oil

1. Make Vegan Parmesan Cheese (see options): Combine cashews, yeast, and turmeric in the bowl of a food processor. Process for 1 minute, or until the mixture is coarsely chopped.

2. Add garlic and pine nuts and process for 20 seconds. Don't overprocess or the yeast will become gummy.

3. Add 2 cups of the basil and pulse for 10 seconds. Stop and scrape down the sides of the bowl. Add salt and remaining 2 cups of basil. With the motor running, slowly add oil through the opening in the lid until the pesto reaches the desired consistency.

TO USE

My favorite way to enjoy pesto is to spread it on toasted multigrain bread, add a thick heirloom tomato slab, and top with Vegan Parmesan Cheese (page 39). Pesto can also be thinned with olive oil and lemon juice and used as a dressing for cooked pasta, warm or cold salads, and cooked vegetables.

TO STORE

Pesto keeps in a covered container in the refrigerator for up to 1 week.

YOU'VE GOT OPTIONS

In this recipe, Vegan Parmesan Cheese (page 39) is made in step 1, so if you have 1¼ cups already made, omit the first three ingredients and the first step. Add cheese to the bowl of a food processor and continue with steps 2 and 3.

MAC 'N' CHEESE

MAKES 6 SERVINGS

1 medium sweet potato, unpeeled

3 cups dried macaroni (about 9 ounces)

1 teaspoon sea salt

3 tablespoons extra-virgin avocado oil or olive oil

1 large onion, chopped

2 cloves garlic, finely chopped

½ cup raw cashews

¼ cup nutritional yeast

1 tablespoon balsamic vinegar

1 tablespoon coconut sugar (optional)

GARNISH (OPTIONAL)

6 tablespoons Vegan Parmesan Cheese (page 39), or store-bought, or 1 tablespoon smoky or sweet paprika

12 slices Vegan Bacon, Try it! recipe (page 87) or store-bought (optional)

TO SERVE

Spoon into six dishes and garnish each with 1 tablespoon vegan Parmesan cheese or ½ teaspoon paprika (if using). Add 2 slices vegan bacon (if using) to each dish.

1. Preheat oven to 375°F. Line a baking sheet with parchment paper. Cut potato in half lengthwise and place cut side down on baking sheet. Bake for 30 minutes, or until tender when pierced with the tip of a knife.

2. Meanwhile, bring a large saucepan of water to a boil over high heat. Add macaroni and salt and stir. Bring back to a boil, then reduce heat to medium-low and lightly boil for 6 to 8 minutes, until macaroni is al dente. Drain and rinse the macaroni and set aside.

3. In the same saucepan, heat oil over medium-high heat. Add onion and cook, stirring frequently, for 5 minutes. Add garlic and cashews and cook, stirring frequently, for 3 minutes, or until garlic is fragrant and nuts are lightly browned.

4. Pour 2 cups water into a blender jug. Peel sweet potato halves, discard skin, and add flesh to the jug. Scrape onion-garlic-cashew mixture into jug. Add yeast, vinegar, and sugar (if using). Blend on high for 1 minute, or until sauce is smooth.

5. Pour sauce into the same saucepan used to cook the onion. Add macaroni and toss to mix well. Bring to a simmer over medium-high heat and heat through (about 1 minute), stirring frequently.

PAT'S TIP: The mushroom bacon makes this dish exceptional, and if you don't already have some made, it's just a little extra effort, requiring only four ingredients and utilizing the hot oven used to cook the potato. When the potato comes out, transfer the mushroom slices onto the same baking sheet and bake, following directions in the recipe (page 87).

YOU'VE GOT OPTIONS

If your comfort mac 'n' cheese is a baked version with a crunchy top, we've got you covered: Preheat oven to 375°F. After step 5, scrape the macaroni into a large, lightly oiled 8-cup-capacity heatproof dish. Melt 2 tablespoons olive oil in a skillet over medium heat. Stir in ½ cup chopped walnuts or pecans (you choose) and ½ cup panko or oatmeal. Cook, stirring frequently, for 5 minutes or until lightly browned. Spread topping evenly over macaroni and slide onto the middle rack of the oven. Bake for about 7 minutes, or until topping is crisp and macaroni is bubbling.

Try it! VEGAN BACON

MAKES 10 TO 12 SLICES, EASILY DOUBLED

¼ cup soy sauce or tamari

2 tablespoons pure maple syrup

1 teaspoon toasted sesame oil

1 large portobello mushroom

Coarse sea salt (optional)

TO STORE

Vegan bacon keeps in a covered container in the refrigerator for up to 1 week.

TO USE

Vegan bacon is delicious in wraps and burritos, as well as chopped and added to Tofu Scramble (page 77). It's also a great garnish for any "Dinner in a Bowl" (see page 83) or "Mains and Core Meals" (see page 173) dish.

1. Preheat oven to 375°F. Line a rimmed baking sheet with parchment paper.

2. Combine soy sauce, maple syrup, and sesame oil in a shallow dish or pie plate. (Tip: This is enough marinade for several mushrooms.)

3. Wash mushroom under cool water and pat dry. Remove stem and cut into ¼-inch slices. Marinate in soy sauce mixture for 10 to 30 minutes (or overnight in the refrigerator), turning slices over once or twice.

4. Lift slices onto prepared baking sheet with a fork, letting marinade drain off. Bake for 20 minutes. Turn slices over and bake for 10 minutes more. Grind coarse sea salt over bacon, if desired.

VEGETABLE STIR-FRY WITH TEMPEH

MAKES 4 SERVINGS

2 tablespoons balsamic vinegar

2 tablespoons soy sauce or tamari

2 cloves garlic, minced

1 (8.5-ounce) package tempeh, thawed if frozen

3 tablespoons extra-virgin avocado oil, divided

1 medium onion, chopped

¼ head red cabbage, cored and chopped

1 medium carrot, chopped

½ red bell pepper, thinly sliced

1 cup halved red or green seedless grapes or grape tomatoes

2 cups cooked or 1 (15-ounce) can white beans, rinsed and drained

1 lightly packed cup baby or chopped, fresh spinach

4 servings cooked noodles or rice (optional), for serving

GARNISH (OPTIONAL)

¼ cup chopped pistachios

TO SERVE

If using noodles or rice, spoon into four bowls. Spoon vegetables over and garnish each bowl with 1 tablespoon pistachios (if using).

1. Combine vinegar, soy sauce, and garlic in a bowl. Cut tempeh into 1-inch cubes and stir into soy sauce mixture. Set aside to marinate for at least 5 minutes.

2. Meanwhile, heat 2 tablespoons of the oil in a wok or large skillet over medium-high heat. Add onion and cabbage and cook, stirring frequently, for 4 minutes. Add carrot and pepper and cook, stirring frequently, for 3 minutes.

3. Stir in tempeh and sauce mixture. Add grapes, beans, and spinach and cook, stirring frequently, for 3 minutes, or until heated through.

VEGGIE FRIED RICE

MAKES 4 SERVINGS

½ teaspoon sea salt

1½ cups white or brown rice

2 tablespoons extra-virgin olive oil

2 medium onions, chopped

2 tablespoons toasted sesame oil

¼ head green cabbage, chopped (see options)

1 medium carrot, shredded (see options)

2 tablespoons soy sauce or tamari

1 cup peas, fresh or frozen

½ cup salted cashews

GARNISH (OPTIONAL)

4 sprigs parsley

1. Bring 3 cups water and salt to a boil in a large saucepan. Stir in rice, cover, reduce heat to medium-low, and simmer for 20 minutes, or until rice is tender. Remove from heat, stir with a fork, and set aside.

2. Heat olive oil over medium heat in a large wok or skillet. Add onions and cook, stirring frequently, for 5 minutes. Drizzle sesame oil over onions, stir, and add cabbage and carrot. Cook, stirring frequently, for 5 minutes, or until onions are soft and cabbage is crisp-tender.

3. Add soy sauce and peas. Cook, stirring constantly, for 1 minute, or until peas are crisp-tender. Add rice and toss to mix.

TO SERVE

Divide rice among four bowls. Sprinkle 2 tablespoons cashews over each bowl and garnish with a sprig of parsley (if using).

TO USE

Serve this as the base for any "Dinner in a Bowl" recipe: add cooked or raw veggies, cooked lentils or beans, chopped dried fruit, nuts, and/or seeds, and drizzle with Chipotle Dipping Sauce (page 48) or Peanut Sauce (page 29).

YOU'VE GOT OPTIONS

Use any vegetable in this delicious rice dish:

- Use chopped kale or bok choy instead of cabbage.

- Add 1 cup cooked beans or lentils, sliced mushrooms, or zucchini.

- Chop up ½ red bell pepper to replace the carrot.

CASHEW AND COCONUT CURRY NOODLE BOWL

MAKES 4 SERVINGS

3 tablespoons extra-virgin avocado oil

2 tablespoons Curry Spice Blend (page 35), or store-bought

1 medium onion, chopped (see options)

¼ head cabbage, chopped (see options)

1 cup (1-inch) cubed squash (see options)

1 medium carrot, chopped

1 (13.5-ounce) can coconut milk

¼ cup raisins (see options)

8 ounces rice vermicelli noodles

2 lightly packed cups baby or chopped, fresh spinach

Sea salt

½ cup raw cashews, for garnish

1. Heat oil in a wok or large skillet over medium-high heat. Add spice blend and cook, stirring constantly, for 30 seconds. Add onion and cook, stirring frequently, for 5 minutes, or until tender.

2. Add cabbage, squash, and carrot. Stir well to coat. Add coconut milk and raisins and bring to a boil. Reduce heat to medium and simmer, stirring occasionally, for 12 minutes, or until vegetables are crisp-tender. Add ¼ cup water if mixture is too thick or dry as it cooks.

3. Cook noodles: Place in a large heatproof bowl. Pour boiling water over the top of noodles until they're covered completely. Set aside to stand for about 4 minutes, or until al dente. Drain and rinse with cool water.

4. Add spinach to vegetables in the wok and stir to incorporate. Cook, stirring constantly, for 1 to 2 minutes, or until wilted. Taste and add salt if required.

TO SERVE

Divide noodles among four bowls and spoon vegetable curry mixture over. Sprinkle 2 tablespoons cashews over each bowl.

YOU'VE GOT OPTIONS

- All kinds of squash work in this curry: acorn, butternut, hubbard, or turban are just a few of the varieties to try.

- Try swapping cubed turnip or rutabaga for all or half of the squash.

- Try a leek in place of or in addition to the onion: clean and trim the root end, chop the white and most of the green parts, and add in step 1.

- One cup broccoli or cauliflower florets may be used instead of the cabbage.

- Any dried fruit can be substituted for the raisins.

SQUASH, BEAN, AND CORN COMFORT BOWL

MAKES 4 SERVINGS

1 small acorn or butternut squash

3 tablespoons extra-virgin coconut oil

1 medium onion, thinly sliced

2 cloves garlic, finely chopped

2 cups chopped kale (see options)

1 cup frozen yellow wax beans (see options)

1 cup frozen corn kernels (see options)

Sea salt

½ cup Peanut Sauce (page 29), or store-bought, or Chipotle Dipping Sauce (page 48), or store-bought

GARNISH (OPTIONAL)

¼ cup dried cranberries or cherries

¼ cup toasted pine nuts

1. Preheat oven to 375°F. Line a rimmed baking sheet with parchment paper.

2. Cut squash in half lengthwise. Remove and discard seeds. Place cut sides down on prepared baking sheet. Bake for 25 to 35 minutes, until flesh is tender. Set aside on a cooling rack for 12 minutes, or until cool enough to handle.

3. Meanwhile, heat oil in a large skillet over medium heat. Break onion slices into rings and add to skillet. Cook, stirring frequently, for 5 minutes, or until onion rings are soft and fragrant. Add garlic and kale and cook for 4 minutes, or until kale is wilted. Add beans and corn and cook, stirring occasionally, for 2 minutes or until warmed through. Taste and add salt if required. Set aside until squash is cooked and cooled.

4. Remove skin from squash by sliding a large spoon between the flesh and the skin of each half. Discard skin and cut each half into four slices lengthwise.

TO SERVE

Divide kale mixture among four bowls. Arrange 2 slices of squash on top of each and drizzle 2 tablespoons peanut sauce over each. Sprinkle with cranberries and pine nuts (if using).

YOU'VE GOT OPTIONS

- Kale keeps its resilient texture even when cooked, but frozen, chopped kale is softer. Even still, if it's not your thing, substitute spinach, bok choy, or Swiss chard.

- Try lima beans or peas in place of the yellow wax beans.

- 2 cups of frozen mixed vegetables can replace the beans and corn.

QUINOA POWER BOWL WITH CAULIFLOWER AND CHICKPEAS

MAKES 4 SERVINGS

SEE PHOTOGRAPH ON PAGE X

1 tablespoon extra-virgin olive oil

1 cup quinoa

2 cups Vegetable Broth (page 125), or store-bought, or water

½ head cauliflower, cut into 1-inch florets

12 to 16 fresh asparagus spears or 2 medium zucchini, cut into spears

2 cups cooked or 1 (15-ounce) can chickpeas, rinsed and drained

3 tablespoons softened extra-virgin coconut oil

1 tablespoon Curry Spice Blend (page 35), or store-bought

½ teaspoon sea salt

¼ teaspoon pepper

¼ cup coarsely chopped walnuts

1 cup Avocado Dip (page 45), or store-bought guacamole, for serving

1. Preheat oven to 425°F. Line a rimmed baking sheet with parchment paper.

2. Cook the quinoa: Heat olive oil in a saucepan over medium-high heat. Add quinoa and toast, stirring frequently, for 2 minutes, or until lightly browned. Add broth and bring to a boil. Cover, reduce heat to low, and simmer for 15 to 20 minutes, until quinoa is cooked through. Remove lid, fluff with a fork, and set aside.

3. Toss cauliflower, asparagus, chickpeas, coconut oil, spice blend, salt, and pepper together in a large bowl. Spread on prepared baking sheet in one layer. Roast for 15 minutes. Stir, then add walnuts. Return to oven and roast for 15 minutes more, or until nuts are toasted and cauliflower is crisp-tender.

TO SERVE

Divide quinoa among four bowls. Spoon cauliflower mixture over quinoa and spoon about ¼ cup avocado dip in the center. Garnish with your choice of toppings (see options).

YOU'VE GOT OPTIONS

As with all of the recipes in this section, you can change up the grain, the vegetables, the garnish, and the sauce or dressing. For garnish or toppings, try any or all of the following:

- ½ cup Vegan Parmesan Cheese (page 39), or store-bought

- Sliced avocado or tomato

- Shredded beets, carrots, rutabagas, and/or turnips

REFRIED BEAN AND RICE BOWL

MAKES 4 SERVINGS

3 tablespoons extra-virgin olive oil, divided

1 medium onion, chopped

1 red bell pepper, chopped

2 cups chopped broccoli or cauliflower

1 handful snow peas or green beans, roughly chopped

2 cloves garlic, chopped

2 cups cooked rice, Try it! recipe (page 96)

2 tablespoons soy sauce or tamari

1 cup Vegan Refried Beans, Try it! recipe (page 97) or store-bought

½ cup chopped raw cashews

GARNISH (OPTIONAL)

Hot sauce or chili sauce

TO SERVE

Spoon rice mixture into four bowls and spoon ¼ cup refried beans into the center of each bowl. Garnish each bowl with 2 tablespoons cashews. Serve with hot sauce or chili sauce on the side if desired.

1. Heat 2 tablespoons of the oil in a large skillet or wok over medium heat. Add onion and pepper and cook, stirring frequently, for 5 minutes, or until soft and fragrant. Add broccoli, snow peas, and garlic and cook, stirring frequently, for 2 minutes, or until garlic is soft and fragrant.

2. Add remaining tablespoon of oil and cooked rice and stir well to coat the grains. Add soy sauce and cook, stirring constantly, until rice is evenly brown and heated through.

Try it! HOW TO COOK RICE

½ teaspoon sea salt

1 cup long-grain white rice

1. Bring 2 scant cups water and salt to a boil in a medium saucepan over high heat. Stir in the rice and stir until water comes to a simmer. Cover and reduce heat to low or medium-low to keep the rice simmering. Simmer, covered, for about 20 minutes (start checking to see if rice is tender and all of the liquid is absorbed at about 17 minutes).

2. When rice is tender, turn off the heat, remove the lid, and stir with a fork. Let it sit on the warm burner for 2 to 4 minutes to finish absorbing any liquid.

   Note: Brown rice, mahogany rice, and wild rice may take more time to simmer until tender. Follow directions on the package for optimum amount of water and rice to use. To make 3 cups cooked rice, use 3 cups water and 1½ cups rice.

Try it!
HOW TO COOK DRIED BEANS

1 cup (½ pound) dried pinto beans or other variety beans

1. Place beans in a large saucepan. Cover with water and bring to a boil over high heat. Lower heat and simmer for 2 minutes.

2. Turn heat off. Cover and let sit on the burner for 2 hours or overnight. Drain and rinse thoroughly. Return beans to the pot and cover with water. Bring to a boil, reduce heat to simmer, and cook for 30 to 50 minutes, until tender (check after 30 minutes and keep checking every 5 or 10 minutes until beans are tender). Drain (if making Vegan Refried Beans, reserve 2 cups cooking liquid) and rinse.

Try it!
VEGAN REFRIED BEANS

MAKES 4 SMALL SERVINGS

1 (15-ounce) can cooked red beans with liquid (see options)

3 tablespoons extra-virgin avocado oil

1 medium onion, chopped

2 cloves garlic, minced

1 jalapeño pepper, minced, or 1 canned chipotle pepper in adobo sauce, minced

½ teaspoon sea salt

1. Drain beans using a fine-mesh strainer over a bowl to reserve the liquid. Set beans and liquid aside.

2. Heat oil in a large skillet or saucepan over medium-high heat. Add onion and cook, stirring frequently, for 5 minutes, or until soft and fragrant. Stir in garlic, jalapeño, and salt and cook, stirring constantly, for 2 minutes, or until garlic is fragrant. Add drained beans, remove pan from the heat, and mash using a potato masher. Add reserved cooking liquid to thin the beans to the desired consistency.

3. Season to taste with salt.

YOU'VE GOT OPTIONS

- For convenience, keep cans of cooked beans—black, kidney, red, pinto, white, chickpeas—and lentils on hand. See page 9 for health issues about canned food.

- For greater economy, you can buy dried beans and store them almost forever. See *Try it!* recipe (page 96) for how to cook dried beans.

- Typically, red, kidney, or pinto beans are used to make refried beans, but you can use any cooked bean: black, kidney, white, navy, black-eyed peas, or even chickpeas (although the texture will be slightly drier).

SPRING VEGGIE BOWL WITH MAPLE SYRUP VINAIGRETTE

MAKES 4 SERVINGS

4 cups (1-inch) cubed new potatoes

2 cups roughly chopped broccoli

½ teaspoon sea salt

3 tablespoons extra-virgin avocado oil, divided

1 leek, white and green parts, sliced (see options)

1½ cups sliced mushrooms (see options)

1 cup roughly chopped snow peas (see options)

1 cup fresh peas

½ cup roughly chopped walnuts

Sea salt

½ cup Maple Syrup Vinaigrette, Try it! recipe (page 99)

GARNISH (OPTIONAL)

¼ cup sesame seeds

1. Cover potatoes and broccoli with 5 to 6 cups water in a large saucepan. Add salt and bring to a boil over medium-high heat. Cover, reduce heat to medium-low, and simmer for 8 to 12 minutes, until fork tender. Drain and rinse with cold water in a colander.

2. Meanwhile, heat 2 tablespoons of the oil in a large skillet or wok over medium-high heat. Add leek and cook, stirring frequently, for 5 minutes. Add mushrooms and cook, stirring frequently, for 5 minutes. Stir in snow peas.

3. Add remaining tablespoon of oil to the pan and stir in cooked potatoes and broccoli, peas, and walnuts. Cook, stirring frequently, for 3 to 5 minutes, until peas are cooked. Taste and add salt if required.

TO SERVE

Spoon potato mixture into four bowls. Drizzle 2 tablespoons vinaigrette and 1 tablespoon sesame seeds (if using) over each.

YOU'VE GOT OPTIONS

- I love cooking with shiitake and Lion's Mane mushrooms for their medicinal value, but you can use cremini or other mushroom available.

- ½ cup chopped red or yellow onion can replace the leek or be added in addition to the leek in step 2.

- Try lots of different green vegetables: diced zucchini or Brussels sprouts in place of the broccoli, spinach or other greens in place of the snow peas.

- Make it a winter root vegetable dish by swapping chopped or shredded carrots, parsnips, or rutabagas for the mushrooms.

- I love the vinaigrette, but Basil Pesto (page 85) is also nice with this bowl, as are Chipotle Dipping Sauce (page 48), Tahini Sauce (page 32), and Peanut Sauce (page 29).

- If you have it, toss in 3 tablespoons fresh thyme or 1 tablespoon dried. (Lemon thyme is divine!)

- Make extra for leftovers because this makes an excellent side for Tofu Scramble (page 77) or stuffing for Breakfast Burritos (page 80).

Try it!
MAPLE SYRUP VINAIGRETTE

MAKES ¼ CUP, EASILY DOUBLED

2 tablespoons apple cider vinegar

2 tablespoons pure maple syrup

1 tablespoon sesame oil

1 tablespoon soy sauce or tamari

Combine vinegar, maple syrup, sesame oil, and soy sauce in a clean jar with a tight-fitting lid. Shake well.

TO STORE
Vinaigrette keeps in a covered container in the refrigerator for up to 1 week.

SWEET POTATO AND WHITE BEAN BURRITO BOWL

MAKES 4 SERVINGS

1 medium sweet potato, peeled and cut into 1-inch cubes

1 medium onion, cut into wedges

2 cloves garlic

2 large or 4 small tomatoes, cored and halved

3 tablespoons extra-virgin avocado oil

½ to 1 tablespoon chili seasoning

1 teaspoon Curry Spice Blend (page 35), or store-bought

½ teaspoon sea salt

1 (15-ounce) can white beans, drained and rinsed (see options)

2 cups halved red seedless grapes

¼ cup chopped fresh cilantro or parsley

1 tablespoon freshly squeezed lime juice

2 cups cooked rice (see page 96), for serving

½ cup Chipotle Dipping Sauce (page 48), or store-bought (optional)

GARNISH (OPTIONAL)

½ ripe avocado, sliced

1. Preheat oven to 375°F.

2. Combine sweet potato, onion, garlic, and tomatoes in a roasting pan. Drizzle oil over them and sprinkle with chili seasoning, spice blend, and salt. Toss to coat.

3. Roast for 30 minutes, or until potatoes are tender and lightly browned. Remove from oven and add beans, grapes, and cilantro to pan. Sprinkle lime juice over and toss well.

YOU'VE GOT OPTIONS

- Although this is a bowl recipe, you can wrap it up to go: combine rice and sweet potato mixture together, spoon about ½ cup into the center of a 10-inch tortilla, top with avocado slices, and wrap as you would a burrito (see page 80).

- If you wish to cook dried white beans, see instructions on page 96. Use 2 cups cooked beans to replace the canned beans.

- If you have it, toss in ¼ cup chopped fresh savory or oregano (or 2 tablespoons dried).

TO SERVE

Divide rice among four bowls and top with potato mixture. Garnish each bowl with avocado slices if desired. Drizzle 2 tablespoons dipping sauce (if using) over each bowl.

TWO-BEAN CHILI

MAKES 6 TO 8 SERVINGS

2 tablespoons extra-virgin olive oil

1 medium onion, chopped

1 red bell pepper, chopped

3 cloves garlic, finely chopped

2 (12-ounce) cans beer or 3 cups
  Vegetable Broth (page 125), or
  store-bought

2 medium carrots, chopped

1 cup chopped cauliflower

1 jalapeño pepper, finely chopped

¼ cup chopped fresh cilantro or parsley

2 tablespoons chopped fresh thyme or
  savory

2 tablespoons rice vinegar

1 tablespoon coconut sugar (optional)

1 tablespoon ground cumin

1 teaspoon ground chipotle pepper

1 teaspoon sea salt

2 cups Vegan Refried Beans (page 97) or
  1 (14-ounce) can vegetarian refried
  beans (see options)

2 cups cooked kidney beans (see page 96),
  or 1 (14-ounce) can kidney beans

TO SERVE
Ladle into bowls and see
options for toppings.

1. Heat oil in a large pot over medium heat. Add onion and cook, stirring frequently, for 5 minutes. Add bell pepper and garlic and cook, stirring frequently, for 5 minutes, or until vegetables are soft and garlic is fragrant.

2. Add beer and stir for 1 minute to dissipate carbonation. Bring to a boil, then add carrots, cauliflower, jalapeño pepper, cilantro, thyme, vinegar, sugar (if using), cumin, chipotle pepper, and salt. Adjust the heat to keep the chili simmering but not at a full boil. Continue to cook, stirring occasionally, for 15 minutes, or until vegetables are cooked.

3. Add refried beans and stir well into the chili. Stir in kidney beans and simmer for 1 to 2 minutes, until beans are heated through.

YOU'VE GOT OPTIONS

- For convenience, keep cans of cooked beans—navy, kidney, black, pinto, white, chickpeas—and lentils on hand. See page 9 for health issues about canned food.

- For this recipe, you can skip the refried beans and instead use 2 (15-ounce) cans cooked kidney beans. Drain and mash one can to replace the refried beans.

- There are lots of options for garnishing or topping this exceptional chili. Here are a few items to pass for people to choose from:

  - 1 cup Vegan Parmesan Cheese (page 39), or store-bought

  - 1 cup Vegan Yogurt (page 66), or store-bought

  - Lime wedges and/or ¼ cup chopped cilantro

  - Sliced green onions

Asian Noodle Salad, page 106

SALADS

ASIAN NOODLE SALAD

MAKES 4 SERVINGS

SEE PHOTOGRAPH ON PAGE 104

6 ounces rice noodles

2 tablespoons extra-virgin avocado oil

1½ cups sliced shiitake mushrooms (see options)

3 cloves garlic, thinly sliced

1 leek, white and green parts, trimmed and chopped (see options)

2 teaspoons grated fresh ginger (see options)

1 small carrot, shredded

2 tablespoons soy sauce or tamari

2 teaspoons toasted sesame oil

1 head bok choy, sliced (see options)

GARNISH (OPTIONAL)

½ cup sesame seeds

½ cup Peanut Sauce (page 29), or store-bought

TO SERVE

I prefer to add the noodles to the pan with the carrots in step 3 and heat through. Or you can divide the noodles among four plates and spoon the vegetable mixture over them. Garnish each bowl with 2 tablespoons sesame seeds (if using). Drizzle each bowl with 2 tablespoons peanut sauce (if using) or pass the sauce separately.

1. Bring a large pot of salted water to a boil. Add noodles and cook, stirring once or twice, for 4 minutes, or until al dente. Drain and rinse with cold water to stop the cooking. Set aside.

2. Heat oil in a wok or large skillet over medium-high heat. Add mushrooms and cook, stirring frequently, for 5 minutes. Add garlic, leek, and ginger and cook, stirring frequently, for 5 minutes, or until leek is soft and mushrooms give up their juices.

3. Add carrot, soy sauce, and sesame oil and cook, stirring frequently, for 3 minutes, or until carrot is crisp-tender. Add bok choy and cook, tossing with a slotted spoon, for 1 to 2 minutes, until slightly wilted.

YOU'VE GOT OPTIONS

- Shiitake mushrooms contain powerful healing constituents (see page 16), but if they are not available, use cremini or another variety.

- Leeks are awesome in this salad, but if all you have are onions, use one instead. If you happen to have both leeks and onions, use both. One cup chopped shallots can also be swapped for leeks or onions in this recipe.

- Ginger is an essential flavor in Asian recipes and fresh is usually best, but chopped candied ginger may be used in place of fresh. See page 11 for tips on how to store fresh ginger.

- Hot sauce, such as Tabasco, or sriracha may be added by the drop for a spicy-hot zing, or use 1 teaspoon finely chopped fresh chile pepper or chipotle pepper (from a jar of chipotle peppers in adobo sauce).

- Swap 2 cups baby or torn fresh spinach for the bok choy.

CREAMY COLESLAW WITH AVOCADO DRESSING

MAKES 4 TO 6 SERVINGS

SEE PHOTOGRAPH ON PAGE 108

¼ **head purple cabbage (see options)**

¼ **head green cabbage (see options)**

2 **medium carrots, shredded**

2 **green onions, sliced**

1 **beet, shredded (optional)**

½ **to 1 cup Avocado Dressing, Try it! recipe (page 109) or store-bought (see options)**

Sea salt

GARNISH (OPTIONAL)

¼ **cup to 6 tablespoons sesame seeds or shelled raw sunflower seeds**

Thinly slice purple and green cabbage into a large bowl using a mandoline. Add carrots, onions, and beet (if using). Add ½ cup of the dressing and toss well to mix. Add more dressing, if necessary, by the tablespoon until coleslaw is creamy. Taste and add salt if required.

TO SERVE

Divide coleslaw into four or six bowls and sprinkle each with 1 tablespoon sesame seeds (if using).

TO STORE

You can make the shredded ingredients ahead and store in a zip-top plastic bag in the refrigerator for up to 1 week. Once dressing has been added, store coleslaw in the refrigerator for up to 3 days.

YOU'VE GOT OPTIONS

- Combining purple and green cabbage together in a recipe gives you the health benefits of both, but you can use ½ head purple or green cabbage only.

- A mandoline (see page 17) is inexpensive and easy to use for slicing fruit and vegetables, and you can get very thin slices, but you can use a sharp French knife instead to slice the cabbage in this recipe.

- Use mayonnaise in place of the avocado dressing.

Try it!
AVOCADO DRESSING

MAKES 1½ CUPS

3 tablespoons freshly squeezed lemon juice

1 ripe avocado, peeled and pitted

1 clove garlic

1 cup Vegan Mayonnaise (page 43), or store-bought

Place lemon juice in the blender jug. Slice avocado into the jug. Add garlic and mayonnaise and blend on high speed for 1 minute, or until smooth.

TO STORE
Avocado dressing keeps in a covered container in the refrigerator for up to 1 week.

KALE SALAD WITH PEAR AND WALNUTS

MAKES 4 SERVINGS

1¼ cups Vegetable Broth (page 125), or store-bought, or water

½ cup bulgur (see options)

1 tablespoon extra-virgin avocado oil

1 medium onion, chopped

1 to 2 tablespoons Garam Masala Spice Blend (page 25), or store-bought

3 cups chopped kale (see options)

Sea salt

2 pears, cored

2 tablespoons freshly squeezed lemon juice

GARNISH (OPTIONAL)

¼ cup chopped walnuts

1. Combine broth and bulgur together in a saucepan. Bring to a boil over medium-high heat. Cover, reduce heat to low or medium-low, and simmer for 3 minutes. Remove from heat and set aside without lifting the lid.

2. Heat oil in a wok or large skillet over medium-high heat. Add onion and cook, stirring frequently, for 5 minutes. Add spice blend and cook, stirring constantly, for 1 minute, or until well blended.

3. Add kale and bulgur with the cooking liquid. Cover, adjust heat to keep liquids simmering, and cook for about 7 minutes, or until bulgur is tender and liquids have evaporated. Taste and add salt if required.

TO SERVE

Transfer to a serving bowl and slice pears into the salad. Sprinkle lemon juice over the salad and toss to mix. Garnish with walnuts if desired.

YOU'VE GOT OPTIONS

- I get it—some people just don't like kale. Try this delicious salad using chopped Swiss chard, cabbage, bok choy, or other greens instead. If you do use other greens, cook just the bulgur in step 3 and add the greens in the last minute of cooking.

- Bulgur is a great grain (see page 8), but of course you can use rice, wheat berries, or quinoa in its place. You may need to adjust the cooking time in step 3 and add the kale in the last 5 or 6 minutes of cooking.

MOROCCAN POTATO SALAD

MAKES 4 SERVINGS

3 cups (1-inch) cubed potatoes

½ teaspoon sea salt

2 tablespoons extra-virgin avocado oil

1 medium onion, chopped

2 cloves garlic, finely chopped

1 tablespoon Garam Masala Spice Blend (page 25), or store-bought

2 to 4 tablespoons extra-virgin olive oil

2 to 3 tablespoons freshly squeezed lemon juice

Sea salt

GARNISH (OPTIONAL)

1 tablespoon sweet or smoked paprika

TO SERVE

Toss the potato salad in the saucepan. Transfer to individual bowls or a serving bowl and sprinkle with paprika if desired. Serve warm.

1. Cover potatoes with 4 or 5 cups water in a saucepan. Add salt and bring to a boil. Cover, reduce heat to medium-low, and simmer for 8 to 12 minutes, until potatoes are fork-tender. Drain and rinse with cold water to stop the cooking. Set aside.

2. Heat avocado oil in the same saucepan over medium-high heat. Add onion and cook, stirring frequently, for 5 minutes. Add garlic and spice blend and cook, stirring frequently, for 3 minutes, or until garlic is soft and fragrant.

3. Add cooked potatoes, 2 tablespoons olive oil, and 2 tablespoons lemon juice and toss to coat. Taste and add salt and more olive oil and/or lemon juice if needed.

SPRING SALAD WITH MISO DRESSING

MAKES 4 SERVINGS

2 tablespoons extra-virgin avocado oil

1 tablespoon grated fresh ginger

1 clove garlic, minced

1 cup whole-grain barley (see options)

3 cups Vegetable Broth (page 125), or
   store-bought, or water

1 bunch fresh asparagus (about 6 ounces)
   (see options)

2 cups baby spinach leaves

1 cup roughly chopped snow peas

1 firm ripe avocado, peeled and pitted

⅓ cup Miso Dressing, Try it! recipe
   (page 116) (see options)

GARNISH (OPTIONAL)

½ cup chopped toasted pistachios (see
   options)

1. Heat oil in a saucepan over medium-high heat. Add ginger and garlic and cook, stirring constantly, for 1 minute. Add barley and cook, stirring frequently, for 2 minutes. Add broth and bring to a boil. Cover, reduce heat to medium-low, and simmer for 25 minutes, or until barley is tender. Drain if any liquid remains and set aside.

2. Bring a medium-sized pot of salted water to a boil. Trim asparagus and cut into 1½- to 2-inch pieces. Blanch asparagus in boiling water for 1 minute, or until bright green and tender-crisp. Rinse under cold water and drain. Set aside.

3. Combine barley, spinach, and snow peas together in a large bowl. Add asparagus and slice in the avocado. Drizzle dressing over the salad and gently toss to coat ingredients.

YOU'VE GOT OPTIONS

- Barley is a great grain for this salad because it adds a chewy texture and nutty flavor. Substitute wheat berries, quinoa, or brown rice if you prefer, but check the package directions for cooking time for those grains in step 1.

- Asparagus is in season in the spring. Seek out fresh, local, and organic if possible. See page 15 for how to shop for asparagus.

- If asparagus is not available, use green beans instead.

- Your favorite nuts may be exchanged for the pistachios (use what you have on hand!)

- You can use Peanut Sauce (page 29), Tahini Sauce (page 32), Chipotle Dipping Sauce (page 48), or Vinaigrette (page 121) instead of the miso dressing.

TO SERVE

Spoon tossed salad into four bowls and garnish each with pistachios (if using). Or pass the salad and the nuts at the table for guests to serve themselves.

Try it!
MISO DRESSING

MAKES ⅓ CUP

3 tablespoons white or brown miso (see page 10)

3 tablespoons mirin (see options)

2 tablespoons soy sauce or tamari

2 tablespoons rice vinegar

1 teaspoon coconut sugar

Combine miso, mirin, soy sauce, vinegar, and sugar together in a small bowl. Whisk using a fork.

TO STORE

Miso Dressing keeps in a covered container in the refrigerator for up to 1 week.

YOU'VE GOT OPTIONS

Mirin is Japanese cooking wine. You can use white or red cooking wine or sherry instead. Or you can omit the mirin and use 3 tablespoons each soy sauce and rice vinegar.

TABBOULEH

¼ teaspoon sea salt

1 cup couscous

1 tomato, chopped

½ small red onion, chopped

½ medium cucumber, chopped

1 (15-ounce) can chickpeas, drained and
  rinsed (optional)

¼ cup chopped fresh mint (see options)

¼ cup chopped fresh parsley

3 tablespoons extra-virgin olive oil or
  flaxseed oil (see options)

2 tablespoons freshly squeezed lemon
  juice

Sea salt and pepper

1. Combine 1 cup water and salt in a saucepan. Bring to a boil and stir in couscous. Cover and remove from the heat. Set aside for 10 minutes, then remove lid, fluff with a fork, and set aside to cool completely.

2. Meanwhile, combine tomato, onion, cucumber, chickpeas (if using), mint, and parsley in a large bowl. Set aside. Whisk together olive oil and lemon juice in a small bowl, using a fork.

3. Drizzle oil mixture over vegetables in the bowl and toss well. Stir in couscous and toss to coat. Season to taste with salt and pepper.

YOU'VE GOT OPTIONS

* Mint gives the tabbouleh a fresh, exotic taste, but if you prefer, omit the mint and use ½ cup chopped fresh parsley (fresh parsley is a must for authentic tabbouleh).

* I have used ½ cup Basil Pesto (page 85) in this salad with great results. Simply toss into the mixture in step 3 and omit or use less olive oil, but keep the lemon juice.

MARINATED TEMPEH WITH SHREDDED BOK CHOY

MAKES 4 SERVINGS

MARINADE (SEE OPTIONS)

¼ cup dry sherry (see options)

¼ cup rice wine vinegar

¼ cup soy sauce or tamari

1 clove garlic, minced

1 tablespoon grated fresh ginger

1 teaspoon toasted sesame oil (optional)

1 teaspoon coconut nectar (optional)

1 or 2 (8.5-ounce) packages tempeh,
    thawed if frozen

SALAD

3 cups shredded bok choy (see options)

2 green onions, chopped

1 medium carrot, shredded

1 cup bean sprouts (see options)

½ red or green bell pepper, chopped

¼ cup cornstarch

TO SERVE

You can cool the thickened marinade or use it right from the pan for a warm salad. Drizzle over vegetables, toss well, and transfer to four bowls.

1. Marinate tempeh: Combine sherry, vinegar, soy sauce, garlic, ginger, sesame oil (if using), coconut nectar (if using), and 2 tablespoons warm water in a shallow pan. Cut tempeh into 1-inch cubes and add to the dish. Cover and set aside on the counter for 2 to 4 hours, stirring occasionally, or let marinate in the refrigerator overnight.

2. Make salad: Combine bok choy, green onions, carrot, bean sprouts, and pepper in a large bowl. Lift tempeh out of marinade (reserve marinade) using a slotted spoon and toss with vegetables.

3. Scrape marinade into a saucepan and whisk in cornstarch using a fork or whisk. Bring to a light boil over medium-high heat. Reduce heat to medium-low to keep simmering and cook, stirring constantly, for 7 minutes, or until thickened.

YOU'VE GOT OPTIONS

- I know, it seems like such a long list of ingredients for the marinade, so for convenience, you can omit the marinade ingredients altogether. Instead, use 1 cup store-bought or homemade Peanut Sauce (page 29) or Chipotle Dipping Sauce (page 48) as the marinade; pour over tempeh and marinate per step 1.

- Dry sherry adds an authentic flavor to the marinade, but you can use soy sauce or tamari instead. If you omit the sherry, the total amount of soy sauce or tamari becomes ½ cup in the recipe.

- Asian greens (bok choy, Chinese cabbage, tat soi, etc.) are best in this salad, but you can use sliced green cabbage, kale, spinach, or even snow peas or broccoli.

WARM CARROT AND LENTIL SALAD

MAKES 4 SERVINGS

1½ pounds fingerling or small potatoes

½ teaspoon sea salt

4 tablespoons extra-virgin avocado oil, divided

1 medium onion, coarsely chopped, divided

2 tablespoons fresh thyme (see options)

1 cup dried small French green lentils (see options)

1 medium carrot, chopped

1 medium zucchini, chopped

⅓ cup Vinaigrette, Try it! recipe (page 121) or store-bought

Sea salt and pepper

GARNISH (OPTIONAL)

¼ cup chopped fresh parsley

2 green onions, chopped

2 tablespoons chopped capers or chopped gherkins

TO SERVE

Transfer salad to serving bowl. Drizzle vinaigrette over and toss to coat. Season to taste with salt and pepper. Garnish with parsley, green onions, and/or capers if desired, or pass garnishes separately.

1. Cook potatoes: Cover potatoes with 4 to 6 cups water in a large saucepan. Add salt and bring to a boil over medium-high heat. Cover, reduce heat to medium-low, and simmer for 15 minutes, or until fork-tender. Drain, rinse, and set aside (using the saucepan lid to cover and keep them warm) in the colander.

2. Meanwhile, heat 2 tablespoons of the oil in a large, deep-sided skillet over medium-high heat. Add ¼ cup of the chopped onion and the thyme and cook, stirring frequently, for 5 minutes. Add lentils and carrot and stir to combine. Add 2½ cups water and bring to a boil. Cover, reduce heat to medium-low, and simmer for 25 to 30 minutes, until lentils are firm but tender. Drain if any liquid remains and set aside.

3. Heat remaining 2 tablespoons of oil in the large saucepan (the one used to cook the potatoes). Add remaining chopped onion and zucchini and cook, stirring constantly, for 5 to 7 minutes, until vegetables are tender. Stir in potatoes and lentils and heat through.

YOU'VE GOT OPTIONS

- If you want convenience, use a 15-ounce can of green or brown lentils, drained, rinsed, and added in step 3. Skip the chopped onions and the thyme in step 2 and use all of both in step 3.

- Fresh herbs are appearing more often in supermarkets and thyme may be available in the produce aisle, but you can use 1 tablespoon dried thyme in this recipe.

- For extra nutrients, toss a cup or two of chopped spinach or other greens into the pan in step 3, just before adding the potatoes and lentils.

Try it! VINAIGRETTE

MAKES ⅓ CUP

¼ cup extra-virgin olive oil, flaxseed oil, or other cold-pressed oil

2 tablespoons red wine, balsamic, or rice wine vinegar

1 tablespoon Dijon mustard

1 tablespoon chopped gherkins (optional)

In a small bowl, combine oil, vinegar, mustard, and gherkins (if using). Whisk together using a fork.

TO STORE

Vinaigrette keeps for up to 2 weeks in a covered container in the refrigerator. Bring to room temperature before using.

Asian Hot, Sweet, and Sour Noodle Soup, page 124

SOUPS

ASIAN HOT, SWEET, AND SOUR NOODLE SOUP

MAKES 4 SERVINGS

SEE PHOTOGRAPH ON PAGE 122

6 ounces rice noodles

2 tablespoons extra-virgin avocado oil

1 medium onion, chopped

1½ cups sliced shiitake mushrooms (see options)

1 medium carrot, shredded

2 cloves garlic, finely chopped

½ cup shredded daikon (optional)

2 teaspoons grated fresh ginger

5 cups Vegetable Broth, Try it! recipe (page 125) or store-bought

¼ cup soy sauce or tamari

2 tablespoons coconut sugar

1 teaspoon sriracha sauce, plus more if desired (optional)

1 head bok choy, sliced (see options) (optional)

Sea salt

GARNISH (OPTIONAL)

1 cup chopped fresh basil

½ cup chopped peanuts

TO SERVE

Ladle soup into four bowls. If desired, garnish each with ¼ cup chopped fresh basil and 2 tablespoons peanuts.

1. Bring a medium-sized pot of salted water to a boil. Add noodles and cook, stirring once or twice, for 4 minutes, or until al dente. Drain and rinse with cold water to stop the cooking. Set aside.

2. Heat oil in a soup pot or large saucepan over medium-high heat. Add onion and cook, stirring frequently, for 5 minutes. Add mushrooms, carrot, garlic, daikon (if using), and ginger. Cook, stirring frequently, for 3 to 5 minutes, until mushrooms are soft and give up their juices.

3. Add broth, soy sauce, sugar, and sriracha (if using) and bring to a boil. Add bok choy (if using), bring back to a simmer, and cook for 6 to 8 minutes, until vegetables are tender. Stir in noodles. Taste and add salt and/or hot sauce if desired.

YOU'VE GOT OPTIONS

- Of course you can use regular button mushrooms in this soup, but why not try shiitake or maitake mushrooms? See page 16 for information on the healing benefits of these mushrooms.

- Replace bok choy with 2 to 3 cups chopped spinach, Swiss chard, or kale.

Try it! VEGETABLE BROTH

SEE PHOTOGRAPH ON PAGE IV

2 to 3 cups vegetable peelings (see options)

4 cloves garlic, unpeeled

2 ribs celery with leaves

1 medium onion, with skin

1 medium carrot, roughly chopped

1 medium parsnip

1 handful fresh or dried parsley sprigs (see options)

1 handful fresh or dried thyme sprigs (see options)

1 fresh or dried bay leaf

1 whole nutmeg seed, crushed

1 teaspoon whole allspice berries

½ teaspoon whole cloves

TO STORE

Pour broth into 1- or 2-cup jars with lids or airtight containers. Refrigerate for up to 3 days or label and freeze for up to 6 months (be sure to leave lots of headspace in the jars or freezer containers).

1. Combine all of the ingredients in the pot of a slow cooker. Add 10 cups cold water, or enough to cover the vegetables by at least 1 inch.

2. Cover, turn heat to medium, and cook for a minimum of 4 hours or overnight.

3. Cool broth and strain liquid into a large bowl or jug, discarding solids.

YOU'VE GOT OPTIONS

- The great advantage of making this broth is that you can use any vegetable and every part of the vegetable, so save everything, from cores to peels. I keep a zip-top plastic bag in the freezer and add vegetable scraps as I cook. When the bag is full, I know that it is time to make vegetable broth.

- If you make juice, save the expelled vegetables and freeze for use in the broth.

- Practically any herb or spice can be added to flavor the broth. If you don't have fresh or dried sprigs, use 3 tablespoons dried leaves or 2 tablespoons dried ground thyme or parsley.

- One healing herb that I always add to my homemade broth is the dried root from the hardy leguminous plant *Astragalus membranaceus*, because it is an immune system booster. I add a couple of the dried roots, available from Asian food markets (they look like tongue depressors), with the vegetables in step 1.

CORN CHOWDER

MAKES 4 SERVINGS

2 tablespoons extra-virgin avocado oil

1 medium onion, chopped

1 clove garlic, chopped

2 teaspoons grated fresh ginger

1 yellow or white potato, chopped

1 small or ½ large sweet potato, shredded

1 tablespoon Garam Masala Spice Blend (page 25), or store-bought

3 cups Vegetable Broth (page 125), or store-bought

1 (19-ounce) can diced tomatoes with liquid

2 cups fresh or frozen corn kernels

1 (14.75-ounce) can cream-style sweet corn (see options)

Sea salt and pepper

GARNISH (OPTIONAL)

¼ cup chopped fresh basil

Sriracha sauce, for serving

1. Heat oil in a soup pot or large saucepan over medium-high heat. Add onion and cook, stirring frequently, for 5 minutes. Add garlic, ginger, yellow potato, sweet potato, and spice blend and cook, stirring frequently, for 2 minutes.

2. Add broth and tomatoes with the liquid and bring to a boil. Reduce heat to medium-low and simmer for 20 minutes, or until potatoes are fork-tender.

3. Add corn kernels and cook, stirring occasionally, for 5 minutes, or until cooked. Stir in canned corn and heat through. Season to taste with salt and pepper.

TO SERVE

Ladle soup into four bowls. If desired, garnish each with 2 tablespoons chopped fresh basil. Pass the sriracha sauce.

YOU'VE GOT OPTIONS

Cream-style corn doesn't actually have any cream in it, but check the ingredients for yourself to make sure you buy a vegan variety. If you prefer, use a 14.75-ounce can of coconut milk instead.

BLACK BEAN SOUP

MAKES 4 SERVINGS

2 tablespoons extra-virgin avocado oil

1 red onion, chopped

2 cloves garlic, chopped

2 medium carrots, chopped

2 cups chopped red cabbage

4 cups Vegetable Broth (page 125), or
store-bought

1 cup chopped kale

2 cups cooked black beans (see page 96)
or 1 (19-ounce) can black beans

Sea salt and pepper

GARNISH (OPTIONAL)

½ cup arame (see page 13)

½ cup Vegan Yogurt (page 66), or store-
bought

¼ cup chopped fresh savory

¼ cup raw pumpkin seeds

TO SERVE

Ladle soup into four bowls.
If desired, garnish each with
2 tablespoons arame, or
2 tablespoons yogurt, or
1 tablespoon chopped fresh
savory, or 1 tablespoon raw
pumpkin seeds.

1. Heat oil in a soup pot or large saucepan over medium-high heat. Add onion and cook, stirring frequently, for 5 minutes. Add garlic, carrots, and cabbage and cook, stirring frequently, for 2 minutes, or until garlic is soft and fragrant.

2. Stir in broth and kale and bring to a boil. Lower heat to medium-low and simmer for 25 minutes, or until vegetables are tender. Add beans and heat through. Add salt and pepper to taste.

CREAM OF MUSHROOM SOUP

MAKES 4 SERVINGS

4 tablespoons extra-virgin avocado oil, divided

1 medium onion, roughly chopped

1 pound cremini mushrooms, quartered (see options)

2 cloves garlic, quartered

1 cup unflavored, unsweetened nondairy milk

1 tablespoon chopped fresh dill (see options)

1 tablespoon soy sauce or tamari

3 tablespoons all-purpose flour or gluten-free flour blend

4 cups Vegetable Broth (page 125), or store-bought, plus more if needed

1 tablespoon freshly squeezed lemon juice

½ teaspoon sea salt, or to taste

GARNISH (OPTIONAL)

½ cup Vegan Yogurt (page 66), or store-bought

TO SERVE

Spoon soup into four bowls. If desired, top each with 2 tablespoons yogurt.

1. Heat 2 tablespoons of the oil in a large saucepan or soup pot over medium-high heat. Add onion and cook, stirring frequently, for 5 minutes. Add mushrooms and garlic and cook, stirring frequently, for 8 minutes, or until soft.

2. Measure milk into a blender jug. Scrape mushroom mixture into jug and add dill and soy sauce. Blend on high for 1 minute, or until mushrooms are chopped. You can stop there to keep the soup chunky, or blend until completely smooth for a creamy soup. Set aside.

3. Add remaining 2 tablespoons of oil to the same saucepan and heat over medium-high heat. Stir in flour and cook until smooth. Add broth and cook, stirring constantly, until the mixture thickens. Stir in mixture from the blender and lemon juice. Heat through. Taste and add salt and/or more broth if desired.

YOU'VE GOT OPTIONS

- Cremini mushrooms are great in this soup because they lend it a rich, dark color, but white mushrooms, shiitake, or other types of mushrooms can be used.

- Don't care for mushrooms? Swap in 2 cups of chopped cauliflower and ¼ cup of the broth in step 1 and proceed with the recipe.

- Fresh dill adds a unique flavor, but thyme or oregano will also work here. Use 1 teaspoon dried if fresh isn't available.

MOROCCAN CARROT SOUP

MAKES 4 TO 6 SERVINGS

4 cups Vegetable Broth (page 125), or store-bought

1 (13.5-ounce) can coconut milk

4 cups sliced or chopped carrots

2 medium onions, chopped

1 cup dried lentils (see options)

2 cloves garlic, finely chopped

1 tablespoon grated fresh ginger

1 tablespoon Garam Masala Spice Blend (page 25), or store-bought

Sea salt and pepper

GARNISH (OPTIONAL)

¼ cup chopped fresh parsley or basil

1. Combine broth, 2 cups water, and coconut milk in the bowl of a slow cooker. Stir in carrots, onions, lentils, garlic, ginger, and spice blend.

2. Cook on low setting for 4 to 6 hours, until vegetables and lentils are tender. Season to taste with salt and pepper.

TO SERVE

Ladle into four to six bowls. If desired, garnish each with 1 tablespoon chopped fresh parsley.

YOU'VE GOT OPTIONS

- This recipe calls for dried lentils because they will cook as the soup simmers—do not use canned lentils here. I love Puy lentils because of their blue-green color and small size, but you can use yellow, brown, orange, or green lentils.

- If you don't own a slow cooker, you can use a soup pot and simmer the soup on the stove. Check after 1 hour; if the lentils and other vegetables are tender, the soup is ready to serve.

SPICED PUMPKIN SOUP

MAKES 4 SERVINGS

2 tablespoons extra-virgin avocado oil

1 medium onion, chopped

1 tablespoon coconut sugar

1 tablespoon Garam Masala Spice Blend (page 25), or store-bought

1 teaspoon grated fresh ginger (optional)

1 teaspoon sea salt (less if using salted broth)

1 (15-ounce) can pumpkin purée

3 cups Vegetable Broth (page 125), or store-bought

1 cup canned coconut milk (see options)

GARNISH (OPTIONAL)

¼ cup coarsely chopped pistachios

1. Heat oil in a large saucepan or soup pot over medium-high heat. Add onion and cook, stirring frequently, for 5 minutes. Stir in sugar, spice blend, ginger (if using), and salt and cook, stirring constantly, for 1 minute.

2. Add pumpkin and half of the broth. Stir well to blend the ingredients. Add remaining broth and bring to a boil, stirring constantly.

3. Reduce heat to medium-low and simmer for 10 minutes. Add milk and simmer for 5 minutes.

TO SERVE

Ladle soup into four bowls. If desired, garnish each with 1 tablespoon chopped pistachios.

YOU'VE GOT OPTIONS

- Fresh ginger is best in this recipe because ground ginger is bitter, so simply omit the ginger if you don't have fresh.

- Coconut milk lends a Thai flavor to the soup, but you can use any unflavored, unsweetened nondairy milk.

TOMATO SOUP

MAKES 8 SERVINGS

¼ cup extra-virgin coconut oil

¼ head green or red cabbage, cored and
cut into 1-inch cubes

1 medium onion, chopped

½ red bell pepper, chopped (see options)

4 cloves garlic, quartered

2 tablespoons chopped fresh rosemary
(see options)

4 cups chopped tomatoes (about 4 large)
(see options)

1 cup Vegetable Broth (page 125), or
store-bought (see options)

2 tablespoons freshly squeezed lemon
juice

Sea salt and pepper

1. Heat oil in a large skillet over medium-high heat. Add cabbage and cook, stirring frequently, for 4 minutes. Add onion and pepper and cook, stirring frequently, for 8 minutes, or until soft. Add garlic and rosemary and cook, stirring frequently, for 2 minutes.

2. Add tomatoes, broth, and lemon juice. Reduce heat, cover, and cook for 15 minutes, or until tomatoes and cabbage are soft. Transfer to a blender and process for 1 minute, or until smooth (you may have to do this in two batches). Return to the pot and heat through. Season to taste with salt and pepper.

YOU'VE GOT OPTIONS

- If you have jarred roasted red bell peppers or canned chipotle peppers, swap in ½ cup chopped for the fresh red bell pepper.

- Fresh rosemary is rich and fragrant in this soup, but you can substitute 1 tablespoon dried.

- Use 1 (28-ounce) can whole tomatoes with liquid in place of the chopped fresh tomatoes.

- You can use store-bought or make your own vegetable broth (page 125), or you can substitute 1 cup tomato juice or tomato sauce in place of the vegetable broth for a tomato-intense soup.

ONION SOUP

MAKES 4 TO 6 SERVINGS

2 tablespoons extra-virgin avocado oil

1 tablespoon miso (see page 10)

4 large onions, thinly sliced

5 cups Vegetable Broth (page 125), or store-bought

½ cup sherry (see options)

1 tablespoon fresh thyme (see options)

1 tablespoon soy sauce or tamari

Sea salt

GARNISH (OPTIONAL)

4 to 6 slices country bread

2 tablespoons extra-virgin avocado oil

¾ to 1 cup shredded vegan mozzarella cheese

1. Heat oil in a large saucepan or soup pot over medium-high heat. Add miso and stir to combine. Add onions and cook, stirring constantly, for 1 minute, or until onions are coated. Cover, reduce heat to low, and sweat the onions for 10 minutes, or until soft.

2. Remove lid and cook, stirring occasionally, for 20 minutes, or until onions are lightly browned and caramelized. Add broth, sherry, thyme, and soy sauce. Increase heat to medium-high and bring to a boil. Reduce heat to medium-low and simmer for 30 minutes. Taste and add salt if desired. You can serve the soup now or garnish with bread and cheese following the "To Serve" steps.

YOU'VE GOT OPTIONS

- Sherry gives the soup an authentic flavor, but you can use 1 tablespoon red wine vinegar in its place, or try using leftover wine instead.

- Fresh thyme lends the soup a Mediterranean flavor, but if only dried is available, dried leaves (as opposed to ground) are preferred; use 1 teaspoon. If you don't have thyme, use oregano.

TO SERVE

Preheat oven to 400°F. Brush bread slices with oil and arrange on a rimmed baking sheet. Bake on the top rack of the oven for 2 to 3 minutes, until lightly browned. Flip and bake for 1 to 2 minutes, until lightly browned on the second side.

Place four or six ovenproof bowls on a rimmed baking sheet. Ladle soup into each bowl and place a toasted slice of bread on the top of each. Sprinkle 3 tablespoons cheese over each bowl. Bake on top rack of the oven for 4 to 5 minutes, until cheese is melted.

RAINBOW VEGETABLE SOUP

MAKES 4 SERVINGS

3 tablespoons extra-virgin avocado oil

1 medium onion, chopped

1 leek, white and tender green parts, chopped (see options)

2 cloves garlic, finely chopped

½ red bell pepper, chopped

1 jalapeño pepper, chopped (optional; see options)

2 medium carrots, chopped

2 ribs celery, chopped

¼ cup cornmeal (see options)

5 cups Vegetable Broth (page 125), or store-bought

2 kale leaves, ribs removed, chopped

1 bay leaf

1 tablespoon chopped fresh rosemary

½ teaspoon sea salt

GARNISH (OPTIONAL)

½ cup Vegan Parmesan Cheese (page 39), or store-bought

1. Heat oil in a large saucepan or soup pot over medium-high heat. Add onion and leek and cook, stirring frequently, for 5 minutes. Add garlic, red bell pepper, jalapeño (if using), carrots, celery, and cornmeal and cook, stirring frequently, for 2 minutes, or until onions and peppers are soft and fragrant.

2. Add broth, kale, bay leaf, rosemary, and salt and bring to a boil. Reduce heat to medium-low and simmer for 45 to 60 minutes, until soup is slightly thickened and kale is tender.

TO SERVE

Ladle soup into four bowls. If desired, sprinkle each with 2 tablespoons vegan Parmesan cheese.

YOU'VE GOT OPTIONS

- You can use 1 teaspoon red pepper flakes in place of the jalapeño.

- For the cornmeal, substitute the same amount of rolled oats, bulgur, white rice, or barley, but keep in mind that they may thicken the soup more than cornmeal would.

ROASTED BEET SOUP

MAKES 6 TO 8 SERVINGS

6 small to medium beets (about 3 pounds), trimmed and quartered (see options)

2 medium onions, trimmed and quartered

6 large cloves garlic, unpeeled

2 tablespoons dried rosemary

3 tablespoons extra-virgin avocado oil

6 cups Vegetable Broth (page 125), or store-bought

Sea salt

GARNISH (OPTIONAL)

¾ to 1 cup Vegan Yogurt (page 66), or store-bought

6 to 8 tablespoons prepared horseradish

1. Preheat oven to 375°F. Spread beets, onions, and garlic evenly in one layer on a rimmed baking sheet. Sprinkle with rosemary and drizzle with oil. Roast for 45 minutes, or until garlic is slightly browned and soft.

2. Bring broth to a boil over medium-high heat in a large saucepan or soup pot. Peel roasted garlic and add with roasted vegetables to the pot. Reduce heat and simmer for 15 minutes, or until beets are soft.

3. Ladle ½ cup of the broth and some of the vegetables into the jug of a blender. Blend at high speed for 1 minute, or until smooth. Empty puréed vegetable mixture into a bowl.

4. Repeat step 3 until all of the vegetables have been puréed. Return to the pot, stir, and heat through. Taste and add salt to taste.

TO SERVE

Ladle soup into six or eight bowls. If desired, top with 2 tablespoons of yogurt and 1 tablespoon horseradish, or pass yogurt and horseradish separately.

YOU'VE GOT OPTIONS

- If you haven't tried roasted beets, you may find that you actually like (dare I say, *love*) the taste—roasting vegetables brings out their sugars, caramelizing the veggies to render them sweet, nutty, and very agreeable.

- Of course, if you like a more rustic, chunky soup, omit steps 3 and 4, but don't forget to taste and add salt if required.

VEGETABLE PHO

MAKES 4 SERVINGS

5 ounces dried soba noodles

2 tablespoons extra-virgin avocado oil

1 medium onion, thinly sliced

6 cups Vegetable Broth (page 125), or store-bought

3 tablespoons soy sauce or tamari

2 tablespoons mirin (see options)

1 tablespoon grated fresh ginger

3 tablespoons miso (see page 10)

1 bunch bok choy, trimmed and chopped (see options)

GARNISH (OPTIONAL)

½ cup chopped peanuts or cashews

2 green onions, thinly sliced

1. Cook noodles: Bring a large saucepan of salted water to a boil over high heat. Add the noodles and cook for 6 minutes, or until al dente. Drain and rinse with warm water. Divide among four serving bowls.

2. Clean the saucepan and heat oil in it over medium-high heat. Add onion and cook, stirring frequently, for 5 minutes, or until soft. Add broth, soy sauce, mirin, and ginger and bring to a boil. Reduce heat slightly to keep broth lightly boiling for 5 minutes.

3. Whisk miso into broth until smooth. Add bok choy and simmer for 1 minute, or until wilted.

TO SERVE

Ladle hot broth over noodles. If desired, serve bowls garnished with 2 tablespoons chopped peanuts and/or 1 tablespoon sliced green onions.

YOU'VE GOT OPTIONS

- Use dry red or white wine in place of mirin, or use 1 tablespoon rice wine vinegar or red or white wine vinegar.

- Bok choy, baby bok choy, and tat soi are Asian greens that work well in pho dishes. You can use 2 cups chopped spinach in place of bok choy.

Linguine with Tomato Sauce, page 146

GRAINS AND SIDES

LINGUINE WITH TOMATO SAUCE

MAKES 4 SERVINGS

SEE PHOTOGRAPH ON PAGE 144

12 ounces quinoa linguine (see options)

2 tablespoons extra-virgin olive oil or avocado oil

1 medium onion, chopped

3 cloves garlic, finely chopped

2 tablespoons chopped fresh rosemary (see options)

1 (28-ounce) can crushed tomatoes with liquid

5 tomatoes, chopped (see options)

½ teaspoon sea salt (see options)

¼ cup chopped fresh parsley

1. Bring a large pot of salted water to a boil. Add pasta and cook, stirring once or twice, for 5 to 7 minutes, until al dente. Drain and rinse with cold water to stop the cooking. Set aside.

2. Make Tomato Sauce: Heat oil in a large skillet over medium-high heat. Add onion and cook, stirring frequently, for 5 minutes. Add garlic and rosemary and cook, stirring frequently, for 2 minutes, or until garlic is soft and fragrant. Add crushed tomatoes with liquid, fresh tomatoes, and salt and cook, stirring occasionally, for 10 minutes, or until sauce is thick. Stir in parsley.

YOU'VE GOT OPTIONS

- Any wheat or wheat-free pasta is delicious with this sauce.

- Substitute 1 tablespoon dried rosemary or Mediterranean Herb Blend (page 147) for fresh rosemary.

- In the winter, when fresh local tomatoes are not available, I use 1 (28-ounce) can diced tomatoes, well drained, instead of the five chopped tomatoes. If using canned tomatoes, you may need to reduce the amount of salt, so taste before adding salt. See page 9 for health information on canned foods.

- For even more veggie goodness, add any of the following in step 2: 1 chopped zucchini, 1 cup sliced mushrooms, 1 chopped red bell pepper.

- For a substantial meal, make Lentil Sliders (page 34) or Fast and Easy Falafel (page 50), add to sauce at the end of cooking step 2, and heat through.

TO SERVE

Divide pasta among four bowls, using tongs to transfer. Spoon hot tomato sauce over pasta and serve immediately.

Try it!
MEDITERRANEAN HERB BLEND

MAKES ¼ CUP

2 tablespoons crushed dried rosemary

1 tablespoon dried chopped oregano

1 tablespoon dried thyme

1 teaspoon dried rubbed sage

Combine rosemary, oregano, thyme, and sage in a bowl and mix well. Transfer to a 1-cup-capacity jar. Cap, label, and store in a cool, dark place for up to 6 months.

MEDITERRANEAN BULGUR

MAKES 4 SERVINGS

2 tablespoons extra-virgin avocado oil

1 red onion, thinly sliced

1 fennel bulb, trimmed, white part thinly
   sliced (see options)

1 medium carrot, shredded

¼ cup slivered almonds

2 cups bulgur (see page 8)

2 cups Vegetable Broth (page 125), store-
   bought, or water

Sea salt

GARNISH (OPTIONAL)

1 cup cherry tomatoes, halved

½ cup pitted green or black olives (see
   options)

¼ cup black or white sesame seeds

1. Heat oil in a large skillet over medium-high heat. Add onion, fennel, carrot, and almonds and cook, stirring frequently, for 5 minutes, or until vegetables are soft and almonds are only slightly browned.

2. Stir in bulgur and broth. Cover and bring to a boil. Remove from heat and let stand for 15 minutes, or until bulgur has absorbed the broth and is fluffy and tender. Add salt to taste. (If using olives, add salt after adding olives.)

TO SERVE

Top the bulgur with cherry tomatoes and olives (if using). Divide bulgur evenly among four bowls. If desired, sprinkle each bowl with 1 tablespoon sesame seeds.

YOU'VE GOT OPTIONS

- Substitute celery for fennel bulb.

- If you just don't like olives, omit them or use halved green or red seedless grapes in their place.

COCONUT GREEN RICE

MAKES 4 SERVINGS

1 (13.5-ounce) can coconut milk

1 cup short-grain brown rice (see options)

2 tablespoons extra-virgin avocado oil

1 small onion, chopped

1 clove garlic, finely chopped

1 cup chopped broccoli

1 tablespoon Garam Masala Spice Blend (page 25), or store-bought

2 cups chopped spinach

¼ cup raisins

Sea salt and pepper

1. Bring coconut milk to a boil in a saucepan over medium-high heat. Stir in rice. Cover and reduce heat to medium-low or low and simmer for 30 minutes. Do not remove the lid during cooking. Stir rice, which will be very wet and soupy. Increase heat and simmer uncovered, stirring frequently, for 10 minutes, or until rice is tender, adding 1 or 2 tablespoons water if needed to keep rice creamy.

2. Meanwhile, heat oil in a skillet over medium-high heat. Stir in onion and cook, stirring frequently, for 5 minutes. Add garlic, broccoli, spice blend, and ¼ cup water and cook, stirring frequently, for 10 minutes, or until broccoli is crisp-tender.

3. Stir rice into broccoli mixture. Add spinach and raisins and cook, stirring constantly, for 2 minutes, or until spinach is wilted. Season to taste with salt and pepper.

YOU'VE GOT OPTIONS

You can use long-grain brown rice, red or mahogany rice, wild rice, or white sticky rice in this recipe, but you will need to adjust the cooking time—less for white rice, more for wild rice.

RAINBOW VEGETABLE RISOTTO

MAKES 4 TO 6 SERVINGS

6 to 8 cups **Vegetable Broth** (page 125), or store-bought

¼ cup extra-virgin avocado oil

1 small onion, chopped

1 red bell pepper, chopped

2 cups **Arborio rice** (see page 8)

1 cup dry white wine

Sea salt

2 cups chopped fresh or frozen (thawed, drained) spinach

½ cup dried blueberries (optional; see options)

GARNISH (OPTIONAL)

½ to ¾ cup **Vegan Parmesan Cheese** (page 39), or store-bought

1. Heat broth to a simmer in a saucepan over high heat. Reduce heat to low and keep warm on a back burner.

2. Heat oil in a large, heavy skillet or saucepan over medium-high heat. Add onion and pepper and cook, stirring frequently, for 5 minutes, or until soft and fragrant. Add rice and cook, stirring constantly, for 3 minutes, or until the grains become translucent around the edges (they will look like glass).

3. Stir in wine and reduce heat to medium-low. Continue to simmer and stir until the wine is absorbed.

4. Using a 1-cup ladle or measuring cup, ladle about 1 cup of hot broth into the rice. Simmer and stir constantly until the broth is absorbed.

5. Add ½ cup of hot broth and simmer, stirring constantly, until broth is fully absorbed. Continue to add broth slowly, waiting until the broth is fully absorbed before adding more, until rice is tender or al dente. This will take about 15 minutes and you may not use all of the broth.

6. Add salt to taste. Stir in spinach and heat, stirring constantly, for about 1 minute, or until wilted. Remove pan from the heat and stir in blueberries (if using).

TO SERVE

Spoon risotto into four to six bowls and garnish each with 2 tablespoons vegan Parmesan cheese (if using).

YOU'VE GOT OPTIONS

- Dried blueberries are optional here, but they are an incredible antioxidant food, helping to prevent all sorts of diseases, and if you buy them for this dish, you will have a supply of them on hand to add to salads and most of the recipes in this book.

- If you have raisins, dried cherries, or dried cranberries, you can use any of them to replace the blueberries.

PASTA PRIMAVERA

12 ounces whole wheat or wheat-alternative penne

2 tablespoons extra-virgin avocado oil

1 leek, chopped (trim off roots and tough outer leaves)

2 cups coarsely chopped fresh asparagus (see options)

1 cup sliced fresh snow peas or frozen peas

1 cup halved cherry tomatoes

¾ cup Basil Pesto (page 85), or store-bought

Sea salt and pepper

GARNISH (OPTIONAL)

¼ cup pine nuts or shelled raw sunflower seeds

1. Bring a pot of salted water to a boil. Add pasta and cook, stirring once or twice, for 5 to 7 minutes, until al dente. Drain and rinse with cold water to stop the cooking. Set aside.

2. Meanwhile, heat oil in a skillet over medium-high heat. Add leek and cook, stirring frequently, for 3 minutes. Stir in asparagus and peas and cook, stirring occasionally, for 6 minutes, or until asparagus is tender and peas are cooked through. Add cherry tomatoes and pesto, stir well, and heat through. Season to taste with salt and pepper.

3. Return penne to the cooking pot. Scrape primavera sauce into the pot and toss to combine.

TO SERVE
Spoon into four bowls and garnish each with 1 tablespoon pine nuts (if using).

YOU'VE GOT OPTIONS

If asparagus is unavailable, use chopped zucchini, green beans, or sliced mushrooms in its place.

SPAGHETTI ALLA PUTTANESCA

MAKES 4 SERVINGS

12 ounces wheat or wheat-alternative
   spaghetti

1 (28-ounce) can diced or crushed
   tomatoes with liquid (see options)

1 cup Olive Tapenade, Try it! recipe
   follows or store-bought (see options)

GARNISH (OPTIONAL)

¼ cup chopped fresh parsley

TO SERVE

Divide spaghetti among four
bowls. Spoon sauce over
spaghetti and garnish each
with 1 tablespoon parsley
(if using).

1. Bring a pot of salted water to a boil. Add spaghetti and
   cook, stirring once or twice, for 5 to 7 minutes, until al
   dente. Drain and rinse with cold water to stop the cooking.

2. Meanwhile, in a saucepan, combine tomatoes with their
   juices and tapenade. Bring to a boil over medium-high
   heat. Reduce heat and simmer for 3 to 5 minutes.

YOU'VE GOT OPTIONS

- Using canned tomatoes is convenient, especially when
  fresh local tomatoes are not in season. I've used whole,
  diced, and crushed canned tomatoes in this dish, and all
  make a delicious sauce. Choose the type that gives you
  the texture you prefer.

- You must like olives if making this dish! One cup of olive
  tapenade is the perfect amount for us, but you might
  start with ½ to ¾ cup and taste to see what amount works
  for you.

Try it! OLIVE TAPENADE

MAKES 2 CUPS

2 (14-ounce) cans pitted black or green
   olives, or 12 ounces pitted Kalamata
   olives

2 cloves garlic

½ cup raw almonds

2 tablespoons chopped fresh parsley

1 tablespoon capers, drained

¼ to ½ cup extra-virgin olive oil

1. Drain olives. Select eight olives, cut in half, and set aside in
   a small bowl for garnish (if desired).

2. Combine garlic and almonds in the bowl of a food
   processor. Blend for 30 seconds. Add unreserved olives,
   parsley, and capers. Pulse two or three times to mix.

3. With the motor running, add oil through opening in lid.
   Pulse just until oil is mixed in well for a chunky texture, or
   pulse for 30 seconds or more for a smooth texture. Scrape
   into a bowl and add reserved olive halves (if using).

TO USE

Olive tapenade is great to have around to use as a dip or a spread for baguettes and crackers.

TO STORE

You need ¾ to 1 cup for Spaghetti alla Puttanasca, so store the remaining amount and use for a spread or dip. Cover tightly or transfer to a 1- or 2-cup- capacity jar with a lid and keep refrigerated for up to 5 days.

BAKED OATCAKES

MAKES 6 TO 9 OATCAKES

2 tablespoons ground flaxseeds

2 cups cooked rolled oats (see options)

1 clove garlic

1 lightly packed cup chopped spinach (see options)

½ cup shredded sweet potato

¼ cup shelled raw sunflower seeds

2 green onions, roughly chopped

1 roasted red bell pepper, chopped

1 tablespoon apple cider vinegar

3 tablespoons coconut flour (see options)

½ teaspoon sea salt

1. Preheat oven to 400°F. Line a rimmed baking sheet with parchment paper.

2. Combine flaxseed and 6 tablespoons water together in a small bowl. Set aside for 10 minutes.

3. Combine oats, garlic, spinach, potato, sunflower seeds, green onions, pepper, vinegar, and flaxseed mixture in a large bowl. You will need a strong arm and a large metal spoon to mix the oats into the other ingredients.

4. Sprinkle flour and salt over and mix well.

5. Scoop up ⅓ cup of batter, form into a tightly packed patty, and transfer to prepared baking sheet. Repeat with remaining batter (you should have six to nine oatcakes). Bake for 15 minutes, flip, and bake for 10 minutes more, or until golden and firm.

TO USE

These oatcakes are brilliant! They can be packed into lunches, stuffed into wraps, and eaten as a snack or breakfast on the run, and they make the perfect accompaniment to any of the bowl dinners or main courses in this book.

TO STORE

Oatcakes keep in an airtight container in the refrigerator for up to 3 days, but I'm sure they won't be around that long.

YOU'VE GOT OPTIONS

- Quinoa is the perfect gluten-free replacement for the rolled oats. See page 94 for how to cook quinoa and use 2 cups cooked quinoa in the recipe. Cover tightly and store in the refrigerator to add to salads, wraps, or other main dishes.

- Omit the spinach or use Swiss chard, kale, or bok choy in its place.

- The coconut flour is a great gluten-free option, but chickpea flour or all-purpose flour can be used.

STOVETOP VEGETABLE LASAGNA

8 or 10 dried lasagna noodles (about 6 ounces), broken in half

8 ounces firm tofu, drained

1 cup Basil Pesto (page 85), or store-bought (see options)

2 tablespoons extra-virgin avocado oil

1 medium onion, chopped

2½ to 3 cups or 1 (28-ounce) can prepared pasta sauce, divided

¼ cup chopped fresh parsley (optional)

GARNISH (OPTIONAL)

¼ cup Vegan Parmesan Cheese (page 39) or vegan mozzarella cheese

1. Place noodles in a shallow heatproof dish and pour 4 to 6 cups boiling water over them. Set aside until ready to use.

2. Mash tofu in a bowl. Add pesto, mix well, and set aside.

3. Heat oil in a large, deep skillet or saucepan over medium-high heat. Add onion and cook, stirring frequently, for 5 minutes, or until soft. Add 1 cup of the pasta sauce and ½ cup boiling water. Lift half of the lasagna noodles out of the water and arrange in one layer over the sauce.

4. Spread pesto-tofu mixture evenly over the noodles and sprinkle parsley over (if using). Lift remaining noodles out of the water and arrange in one layer over pesto-tofu mixture. Pour remaining pasta sauce over all. Cover and bring to a simmer. Reduce heat to medium-low or low and cook, covered, for 25 to 40 minutes, until noodles are tender.

TO SERVE

Remove pan from the heat. If desired, sprinkle vegan Parmesan cheese or mozzarella cheese over the top. Cover and set aside for 5 minutes before serving.

YOU'VE GOT OPTIONS

- Basil Pesto (page 85) is a convenient and delicious ingredient for flavoring the tofu in this dish but you can also use Olive Tapenade (page 154), or store-bought.

- For a veggie boost, add any or all of the following with the onion in step 3: ½ red bell pepper, chopped; 8 mushrooms, your favorite variety, sliced; and/or 2 cloves garlic, finely chopped.

CAULIFLOWER STEAKS

MAKES ABOUT 10 TO 12 STEAKS, EASILY HALVED

1 head cauliflower

2 tablespoons extra-virgin avocado oil, plus more if needed, divided

1 medium onion, chopped

1 clove garlic, finely chopped

1 tablespoon chopped fresh rosemary (see options)

1 tablespoon kosher salt or coarsely ground sea salt, plus more if needed

GARNISH (OPTIONAL)

¼ to ½ cup hummus or Roasted Red Pepper Hummus (page 53), or store-bought

¼ cup Vegan Parmesan Cheese (page 39), or store-bought

1. Preheat oven to 300°F. Line a rimmed baking sheet with parchment paper. Remove the outer leaves, core, and some of the stem from the cauliflower, keeping the head intact.

2. Bring a large pot of salted water to a boil over high heat. Add cauliflower and boil for 3 minutes. Lift out of the water and rinse under cold water. Drain and pat dry.

3. Meanwhile, heat oil in a skillet over medium-high heat. Add onion and cook, stirring frequently, for 5 minutes, or until soft. Add garlic and rosemary and cook, stirring frequently, for 1 to 2 minutes, until garlic is fragrant.

4. Cut cauliflower in half using a serrated bread knife. Position each half cut side down on a cutting board and cut into ¾- to 1-inch-wide slices or steaks.

5. Add a slice to the skillet and cook for 2 minutes, or until lightly browned. Flip over and cook for 1 to 2 minutes, until lightly browned. Remove from the pan and place on prepared baking sheet. Remove onion and garlic from the pan and add to the baking sheet. Place baking sheet in preheated oven.

6. Repeat step 5, adding more oil to the pan as needed, browning remaining slices, and keeping them warm on the baking sheet until all are browned. Sprinkle with salt when all slices have been browned.

TO SERVE

Serve one or two steaks as a side dish with some of the onion, garlic, and herbs, and a dollop of hummus, or sprinkled with vegan Parmesan cheese (if using).

YOU'VE GOT OPTIONS

- Try different herbs and spice blends with this recipe: dried chopped red bell pepper or hot red pepper flakes, Garam Masala Spice Blend (page 25), Curry Spice Blend (page 35), or Mediterranean Herb Blend (page 147).

- One tablespoon lemon juice or soy sauce may substitute for the rosemary.

RAINBOW VEGETABLE STIR-FRY

MAKES 4 SERVINGS

2 tablespoons extra-virgin avocado oil

2 cups roughly chopped dense mixed vegetables, such as carrots, Brussels sprouts, and beets (see options)

2 cups roughly chopped light mixed vegetables, such as onions, spinach, and bell peppers (see options)

2 cloves garlic, finely chopped

½ cup raw almonds or cashews

Juice of ½ lemon

3 tablespoons soy sauce or tamari

2 teaspoons rice vinegar

1 teaspoon toasted sesame oil (optional)

GARNISH (OPTIONAL)

¼ cup nutritional yeast or Vegan Parmesan Cheese (page 39), or store-bought

TO SERVE

Spoon into one serving dish or four side plates and sprinkle nutritional yeast (if using) over the top.

Heat oil in a wok or large skillet over medium-high heat. Add dense vegetables and cook, stirring constantly, for 2 minutes. Add light vegetables and garlic, and cook, stirring constantly, for 3 to 5 minutes, or until vegetables are crisp-tender. Stir in almonds, lemon juice, soy sauce, vinegar, and sesame oil (if using) and cook, stirring constantly, for 1 minute.

YOU'VE GOT OPTIONS

- Dense vegetables include carrots, Brussels sprouts, white and sweet potatoes, broccoli, cauliflower, parsnips, beets, turnips, and rutabagas. Light vegetables include onions, leeks, red and green bell peppers, chile peppers, cabbage, spinach, kale and other greens, celery, radishes, mushrooms, artichokes, and asparagus.

- If you wish to add tofu and turn this into a main dish stir-fry, here's how: Combine 6 to 12 ounces firm tofu, drained and cut into 1-inch cubes, with the lemon juice, soy sauce, vinegar, and sesame oil (if using) from the ingredients list. Set aside for 15 minutes or up to 1 hour. Add to wok in step 2 with all other (lighter) vegetables. Serve over quinoa or another grain. As a main dish, this makes four servings.

- You can add 1 or 2 cups cooked beans or lentils with the light vegetables in step 2.

CHARRED BROCCOLI

MAKES 4 SIDE SERVINGS, EASILY DOUBLED OR HALVED

1 large head broccoli (about 1 pound) (see options)

3 tablespoons extra-virgin avocado oil, divided

1 clove garlic, minced

1 tablespoon Mediterranean Herb Blend (page 147), or store-bought

Grated zest of ½ lemon

½ teaspoon kosher or coarsely ground sea salt

½ teaspoon red pepper flakes (optional)

½ cup peanuts or walnuts

GARNISH (OPTIONAL)

Juice of ½ lemon

¼ cup Vegan Parmesan Cheese (page 39), or store-bought

1. Preheat oven to 425°F. Line a rimmed baking sheet with parchment paper.

2. Wash broccoli and trim and discard any woody part of stem. Cut remaining stem away from florets, leaving florets and about 1 inch of their stems intact. Peel and discard outer skin from cut-off stem and cut crosswise into ½- to 1-inch pieces. Separate or cut florets into 1-inch pieces.

3. Toss together broccoli pieces, 2 tablespoons of the oil, garlic, herb blend, lemon zest, salt, and red pepper flakes (if using) in a large bowl. Spread in one layer on prepared baking sheet.

4. Roast for 20 minutes. Stir and flip broccoli over. Add nuts and spread evenly over the baking sheet. Drizzle with remaining tablespoon of oil and roast for 15 to 20 minutes, until broccoli is crisp-tender and charred around the edges and nuts are golden.

TO SERVE

Scrape broccoli and browned bits into a serving bowl, sprinkle with lemon juice and vegan Parmesan cheese (if using), and serve immediately.

YOU'VE GOT OPTIONS

- Try Brussels sprouts (trimmed and halved) or halved baby bok choy in place of the broccoli (bok choy will take less time roasting in the oven, so test after 10 minutes in step 4).

- Stir in ½ cup dried fruit (blueberries, cherries, raisins, sliced apricots) or sliced green onions as the broccoli comes out of the oven in step 4.

GRILLED BRUSSELS SPROUTS

MAKES 4 SIDE SERVINGS, EASILY DOUBLED OR HALVED

3 cups Brussels sprouts (about 2 pounds), halved (see options)

2 small onions, cut into wedges

1 clove garlic, finely chopped

2 tablespoons extra-virgin avocado oil

½ cup dried fruit (see options)

½ teaspoon kosher salt or coarsely ground sea salt

1. Move oven rack to top position and preheat oven broiler or preheat outdoor grill to medium-high heat. Line a rimmed baking sheet with parchment paper for oven or oil a vegetable grill basket for the barbecue.

2. Toss Brussels sprouts, onions, garlic, and oil together in a large bowl. Spread in one layer on prepared baking sheet or vegetable grill basket. For the oven: Broil for 4 minutes, stir, and broil for 2 minutes, or until tender and slightly charred around the edges. For the barbecue: Grill, stirring occasionally, for 3 to 6 minutes, until tender and slightly charred around the edges.

3. Return to bowl and toss with dried fruit and salt.

YOU'VE GOT OPTIONS

- Try using half Brussels sprouts and half radishes in this recipe.

- Add 1 apple, cored and cut into eight wedges, to vegetables in step 2.

- Use dried blueberries, cherries, raisins, cranberries, or sliced apricots for the dried fruit.

- Or use 1 cup fresh whole fruit: blueberries, strawberries, pitted cherries, or halved pitted peaches, plums, or apricots. Cook with vegetables halfway through cooking time in step 2.

MASHED POTATOES

MAKES 4 SIDE SERVINGS, EASILY DOUBLED OR HALVED

6 red or yellow potatoes (about 4 pounds) (see options)

2 tablespoons extra-virgin olive oil

¾ cup unflavored, unsweetened nondairy milk, heated, plus more if necessary

Sea salt and pepper

GARNISH (OPTIONAL)

½ cup finely chopped onion, browned in 1 tablespoon extra-virgin coconut oil

¼ cup Vegan Parmesan Cheese (page 39), or store-bought

2 tablespoons chopped fresh herbs (see options)

1. Bring a pot of salted water to a boil over high heat. Scrub potatoes and cut small ones in half and large ones into quarters. Add potatoes to boiling water and bring back to a boil. Reduce heat to keep potatoes simmering and cook for 15 minutes, or until fork-tender.

2. Drain potatoes, reserving ¼ cup of the cooking water. Return potatoes to the pot and add oil and ¾ cup of the milk. Mash using a potato masher. If necessary, for a creamy texture, beat in ¼ cup of milk and reserved cooking water. Add salt and pepper to taste.

YOU'VE GOT OPTIONS

- High-starch potatoes such as russets or Yukon gold are the best choice for this because they cook up fluffy and mash easily.

- Chives, basil, thyme, chervil, oregano, or rosemary may be used alone or in combination as a garnish.

TO SERVE

Transfer to a serving bowl and top with onion and/or sprinkle vegan Parmesan cheese and/or herbs (if using) over the top.

SAUTÉED CABBAGE

MAKES 4 TO 6 SIDE SERVINGS, EASILY HALVED

1 small head green cabbage (about 1 pound) (see options)

3 tablespoons extra-virgin avocado oil

2 tablespoons Dijon mustard

1 clove garlic, minced

Sea salt and pepper

½ cup sliced roasted red bell pepper

Juice of ½ fresh lime

GARNISH (OPTIONAL)

1 teaspoon whole caraway seeds

1. Trim away tough outer leaves of cabbage and cut into quarters. Remove and discard tough white core from each quarter. Cut each quarter into ⅛-inch slices.

2. Heat oil in a large, heavy skillet over medium-high heat. Add mustard and garlic and cook, stirring constantly, for 1 minute, or until garlic is soft. Add cabbage and stir to coat. Grind salt and pepper over and cook, stirring frequently, for 5 minutes. Add bell pepper and cook, stirring frequently, for 2 to 3 minutes, or until cabbage is crisp-tender. Drizzle lime juice over and toss to coat.

TO SERVE

Transfer to a serving dish and sprinkle caraway seeds (if using) over the top.

YOU'VE GOT OPTIONS

Try a mixture of 2 cups of any of the following with ½ small head cabbage, trimmed, cored, and sliced: thinly sliced fennel (the white part at the base of the fennel bulb), shredded bok choy, sliced leek, shredded kale, or shredded Swiss chard.

ROASTED ROOT VEGETABLES

MAKES 4 TO 6 SIDE SERVINGS, EASILY HALVED

6 cups vegetable pieces (see options)

4 cloves garlic

2 medium onions, quartered

4 sprigs fresh thyme (see options)

3 tablespoons extra-virgin avocado oil

1 tablespoon balsamic vinegar

Sea salt and pepper

1. Preheat oven to 375°F. Line two rimmed baking sheets with parchment paper.

2. Combine vegetables, garlic, onions, thyme, oil, and vinegar in a large bowl. Grind salt and pepper over and toss to combine.

3. Spread vegetables in one layer on prepared baking sheets. Bake, stirring once or twice, for 40 minutes, or until golden and tender.

TO SERVE
Remove thyme sprigs and transfer to a serving bowl.

YOU'VE GOT OPTIONS

- Use a mixture of any of the following vegetables: carrots, Brussels sprouts, white and/or sweet potatoes, broccoli, cauliflower, parsnips, beets, turnips, rutabagas, leeks, bell peppers, chile peppers, radishes, and mushrooms. Cut the mixture of vegetables in half (Brussels sprouts or small potatoes), into 1-inch cubes or 1-inch pieces and measure 6 cups for this recipe.

- Fresh thyme, oregano, or marjoram sprigs add flavor as the vegetables roast, but if you do not have fresh herbs, use 1 tablespoon Mediterranean Herb Blend (page 147), or store-bought.

BAKED BEANS

MAKES 4 TO 6 SIDE SERVINGS

2 cups dried navy beans (about 1 pound)

3 to 4 cups apple juice, divided (see options)

½ cup ketchup or tomato sauce

¼ cup molasses

2 tablespoons coconut sugar

1 tablespoon balsamic vinegar

1 teaspoon Dijon mustard

2 medium onions, coarsely chopped

Sea salt and pepper

8 to 10 slices Vegan Bacon (page 87), or store-bought, chopped (optional)

PAT'S TIP: This is a slow-cooked dish, and while the oven does most of the work, you do need to set aside some time to soak and cook the beans before baking them in the oven for several hours. The easiest way that I have found is to soak the beans overnight, but you can start in the morning and have baked beans on the table by dinnertime.

This dish is authentic, colonial-style baked beans, and there is no can or convenience you can use to substitute for the real thing.

1. Soak beans: Place beans in a large saucepan and add enough water to cover by 2 inches. Cover and bring to a boil over high heat. Boil for 2 minutes. Turn heat off and let beans sit in the covered pot on the burner for 2 hours or overnight.

2. Cook beans: Drain and rinse beans and rinse the pot. Return beans to the pot and add enough fresh, cool water to cover by 2 inches. Cover and bring to a boil over high heat. Reduce heat to medium-low and simmer, uncovered, for 40 minutes, or until beans are tender but firm.

3. Position rack in middle of the oven and preheat oven to 325°F.

4. Meanwhile, combine 2 cups of the apple juice, ketchup, molasses, sugar, vinegar, and mustard in a saucepan. Bring to a boil over high heat. Stir in onions. Turn off the heat and let sit on the burner.

5. Drain and rinse beans and transfer to a large, ovenproof Dutch oven or bean pot. Add onion mixture and grind salt and pepper over the top. Mix well, cover, and bake for 3 to 4 hours, until beans are creamy, moist, and browned. Stir every hour and add apple juice as beans bake to keep them moist.

6. When beans are baked and removed from the oven, stir in vegan bacon (if using).

YOU'VE GOT OPTIONS

Hard or soft apple cider can stand in for the apple juice, or use a malty beer instead.

THREE BEAN TOSS

2 cups cooked or 1 (19-ounce) can white or black beans

1 cup cooked fresh green bean 1- to 2-inch pieces

1 cup cooked fresh yellow bean 1- to 2-inch pieces

½ red onion, thinly sliced

DRESSING

½ cup extra-virgin olive oil

¼ cup red wine vinegar

2 tablespoons freshly squeezed lemon juice

1 tablespoon white wine (optional)

2 cloves garlic, minced

1 tablespoon Mediterranean Herb Blend (page 147)

½ teaspoon sea salt

GARNISH (OPTIONAL)

¼ cup chopped fresh parsley

TO SERVE

Bring to room temperature. Add parsley (if using) to the bowl and toss to mix before serving.

1. Combine white or black beans, green beans, yellow beans, and onion in a large bowl.

2. Combine oil, vinegar, lemon juice, wine (if using), garlic, herb blend, and salt in a jar with tight-fitting lid. Shake well and pour over bean mixture. Toss well to mix. Cover tightly and chill for 30 minutes or overnight.

Baked Squash Curry, page 174

MAINS AND CORE MEALS

BAKED SQUASH CURRY

1 small acorn or butternut squash

6 cloves garlic, unpeeled

3 tablespoons extra-virgin olive oil, divided

1 medium onion, chopped

⅓ cup cashews

1 tablespoon Curry Spice Blend (page 35), or store-bought

1 cup unflavored, unsweetened nondairy milk

Sea salt and pepper

GARNISH (OPTIONAL)

1 teaspoon red pepper flakes, or more if desired

1. Preheat oven to 375°F. Lightly oil an 11 by 7-inch baking dish.

2. Cut squash in half and scoop out and discard seeds. Cut each half into quarters and peel. Cut each quarter into two or three chunks. Add squash pieces and garlic to prepared baking dish and drizzle with 2 tablespoons of the oil. Bake for 45 minutes, or until squash is tender when pierced with a knife.

3. Meanwhile, make curry sauce: Heat remaining 1 tablespoon of oil in a skillet over medium-high heat. Add onion and cook, stirring frequently, for 3 minutes. Add cashews and spice blend and cook, stirring constantly, for 3 to 4 minutes, until onion is soft and cashews are toasted. Remove from heat and set aside to cool until squash is removed from oven.

4. Pour milk into a blender jug and add onion-curry mixture. Squeeze roasted garlic from skins into the jug, discarding skins. Blend on high for 1 to 2 minutes, until smooth. Season to taste with salt and pepper.

5. Scrape roasted squash into a large serving bowl. Add curry sauce and toss together using two large spoons.

TO SERVE
Garnish with red pepper flakes (if using) or pass flakes separately in a small bowl.

BEAN AND RICE BURRITOS

MAKES 6 BURRITOS

6 (10-inch) soft flour or corn tortillas

2 tablespoons extra-virgin avocado oil

½ medium onion, chopped

½ red bell pepper, chopped (see options)

2 cloves garlic, finely chopped

1 teaspoon chili powder, plus more to taste

½ teaspoon ground cumin

Juice of 1 lime (optional)

2 cups cooked rice (see options)

1 (15-ounce) can black or pinto beans, drained and rinsed

3 tablespoons chopped fresh cilantro or parsley

Sea salt and pepper

GARNISH (OPTIONAL)

Avocado slices

1 cup shredded lettuce

½ cup pitted green or black olives

1½ cups Avocado Dip (page 45), or store-bought guacamole

1½ cups Tomato Salsa (page 78), or store-bought salsa

TO SERVE

If desired, serve each burrito with ¼ cup avocado dip or guacamole and salsa.

1. Preheat oven to 300°F. Wrap tortillas in a moistened kitchen towel or foil and heat in oven.

2. In a large, deep skillet, heat oil over medium-high heat. Add onion and bell pepper and cook, stirring occasionally, for 5 minutes, or until soft. Add garlic, chili powder, and cumin. Cook, stirring constantly, for 2 minutes.

3. Add lime juice (if using), rice, beans, and cilantro and cook, stirring constantly, for 2 minutes, or until heated.

4. Working with one tortilla at a time, spoon ½ cup of the bean-rice mixture over the middle a tortilla leaving an inch at the top and bottom. Grind salt and pepper over. If desired, top filling with avocado slices, lettuce, and/or olives. Fold each end of the tortilla (top and bottom) over the filling. Then fold the right side over the filling and spin the tortilla one-quarter turn to the right so that the filling is closest to you. Using two hands, gently pull the covered filling toward you to make a tight roll. Roll the filled half of the tortilla away from you and over the rest of the tortilla. Secure with toothpicks if you like and cut in half. Fill and wrap remaining tortillas.

YOU'VE GOT OPTIONS

- If you like heat, add a chopped fresh hot chile pepper.

- I like to cook double the amount of rice or grain called for in a recipe so that I will have plenty left over to add to soups, salads, wraps, or burritos. If you have leftover cooked brown or white rice (see page 96) from another dish, use it here. Other grains, such as quinoa, bulgur, spelt kernels, barley, and kamut, also work.

BLACK BEAN BURGERS

MAKES 6 PATTIES

2 tablespoons extra-virgin avocado oil

1 medium onion, chopped

4 cups chopped your favorite mushrooms

2 cloves garlic, finely chopped

2 cups cooked or 1 (19-ounce) can black
    beans, drained and rinsed

1 cup finely chopped walnuts

1 cup rolled oats, spelt flakes, or cooked
    rice

Sea salt and pepper

6 hamburger buns or lettuce cups (see
    serving suggestions)

GARNISH (OPTIONAL)

Peanut Sauce (page 29), or store-bought

Vegan Mayonnaise (page 43), or store-
    bought

Chipotle Dipping Sauce (page 48), or
    store-bought

Basil Pesto (page 85), or store-bought

Enchilada Sauce (page 191), or store-
    bought

Avocado Dip (page 45), or store-bought
    guacamole

Cucumber Relish (page 52)

Lettuce

Ketchup

Mustard

Sliced onions

Sliced tomatoes

1. Preheat oven to 350°F. Line a rimmed baking sheet with parchment paper.

2. Heat oil in a skillet over medium-high heat. Add onion and cook, stirring occasionally, for 5 minutes. Add mushrooms and garlic, reduce heat to medium, and cook, stirring frequently, for 12 minutes, or until tender (mixture should be moist, with no excess liquid from the mushrooms in the pan). Set aside.

3. Meanwhile, mash beans in a large bowl using a potato masher or a food processor (the consistency should be smooth and paste-like, with the occasional whole bean). Add mushroom mixture to beans and mix well. Stir in walnuts and oats. Season to taste with salt and pepper.

4. Using a ½-cup measuring cup, scoop out ½ cup of the mixture, pressing against the side of the bowl. Press the top of the mixture in the cup using a small spatula or the back of a spoon. Invert cup over the baking sheet and use the spatula to ease the mixture onto the sheet. Press into a compact burger shape that is about ¾ inch thick. Measure and form remaining mixture into patties.

5. Bake for 30 minutes, or until firm. Let stand for 7 minutes.

PAT'S TIP: This is perhaps the best "burger" recipe I've ever developed, not only because of its luscious flavor and texture but also because it holds together so well. Burgers are great, but if you're pressed for time, this mixture also makes a perfect vegan loaf. Press into a lightly oiled loaf pan (9 by 5 by 3 inches) and bake for 50 minutes, or until firm. Let stand for 7 minutes before slicing. Serve with any of the sauces in the list of garnishes. Makes six to eight servings.

TO SERVE

Place patties in buns and garnish with desired sauce and condiments, or wrap in lettuce cups and serve with Peanut Sauce (page 29).

TO USE

If you have patties left over, you have instant stuffing for wraps and burritos, or for baking stuffed squash, tomatoes, or bell peppers.

TO STORE

Patties will keep tightly wrapped in the refrigerator for up to 5 days or in the freezer for up to 3 months.

ALMOND, CORN, AND SPELT FRITTERS

MAKES 4 TO 6 FRITTERS

2 tablespoons chia seeds

¾ cup unflavored, unsweetened nondairy milk

½ cup almond flour (see options)

½ cup spelt flour (see options)

2 teaspoons baking powder

½ teaspoon sea salt

2 cups fresh or frozen (thawed) corn kernels

1 zucchini, shredded

¼ cup chopped almonds

3 tablespoons chopped onion or chives

4 tablespoons extra-virgin avocado oil, divided

GARNISH (OPTIONAL)

1 cup Avocado Dip (page 45), or store-bought guacamole

1. Preheat oven to 300°F. Line a rimmed baking sheet with parchment paper.

2. Stir together chia seeds and 3 tablespoons water in a large bowl. Set aside for 10 minutes.

3. Whisk milk into chia mixture using a fork. Whisk almond flour into milk mixture, then whisk in spelt flour, baking powder, and salt. Add corn, zucchini, almonds, and onion and stir to mix.

4. Heat 2 tablespoons of the oil in a large skillet over medium-high heat. Measure ⅓ cup of the fritter batter and drop into skillet. Measure and add two or three more fritter batter portions into the skillet, or as many as the skillet will hold. Cook for 3 minutes, flip, and cook for 2 to 3 minutes, until golden and cooked through.

5. Transfer to prepared baking sheet, cover with foil, and keep warm in preheated oven.

6. Continue to cook remaining batter following step 4, adding more oil to the skillet as required.

TO SERVE

Divide fritters among four plates. Garnish each plate with ¼ cup avocado dip (if using).

YOU'VE GOT OPTIONS

- Almond flour is a great gluten-free flour to use in these fritters, but you can also use a gluten-free blend, unbleached all-purpose flour, or chickpea flour.

- Some gluten-sensitive people tolerate spelt, but if you're not one of them, use 1 cup of any of the alternatives mentioned above.

ROASTED BEETS WITH QUINOA AND SPICED WALNUTS

MAKES 4 SERVINGS

6 medium beets, trimmed and quartered

2 medium onions, quartered

5 tablespoons extra-virgin avocado oil, divided

1 tablespoon Mediterranean Herb Blend (page 147), or store-bought

1 cup whole or coarsely chopped walnuts

1 cup quinoa, rinsed

2 cups Vegetable Broth (page 125), or store-bought, or water

GARNISH (OPTIONAL)

¼ cup Vegan Parmesan Cheese (page 39), or store-bought

TO SERVE

Scrape roasted beets, onions, herbs, walnuts, and juices into a serving bowl. Add quinoa toss to combine. Sprinkle vegan Parmesan cheese (if using) over the top. Or you can divide quinoa evenly among four bowls and top with equal portions of roasted beet mixture.

1. Preheat oven to 375°F. Line a rimmed baking sheet with parchment paper.

2. Toss together beets, onions, 3 tablespoons of the oil, and herb blend in a large bowl. Spread evenly in one layer on prepared baking sheet. Bake for 40 minutes. Stir and add walnuts. Bake for another 10 minutes, or until beets are tender when pierced with the tip of a knife.

3. Meanwhile, cook quinoa: Heat remaining oil in a saucepan over medium-high heat. Add quinoa and toast, stirring frequently, for 2 minutes or until lightly browned. Add broth and bring to a boil. Cover, reduce heat, and simmer for 15 to 20 minutes, until quinoa is cooked through. Remove lid, fluff with a fork, and set aside.

SHAKSHUKA-STYLE TEMPEH

MAKES 4 TO 6 SERVINGS

3 tablespoons extra-virgin avocado oil

1 medium onion, thinly sliced

1 red bell pepper, cut into ½-inch strips

1 jalapeño pepper, cut into ¼-inch slices
(see options)

2 cloves garlic, thinly sliced

1 (8-ounce) package tempeh, thawed if
frozen, cut into 1-inch cubes

1 tablespoon smoked paprika (see options)

2 teaspoons cumin seeds or ground cumin
(see options)

1 (28-ounce) can whole tomatoes with
liquid

1 (6-ounce) jar marinated artichoke
hearts, drained

Sea salt and pepper

GARNISH (OPTIONAL)

½ cup chopped fresh parsley or cilantro

½ cup sliced, oil-cured black olives

TO SERVE

Transfer mixture to a serving
dish or spoon into individual
serving bowls. Sprinkle with
parsley and/or olives if using.

1. Heat oil in a large, deep skillet over medium-high heat.
   Add onion, bell pepper, and jalapeño slices and spread
   evenly over the skillet in one layer. Cook without stirring
   for about 6 minutes, or until vegetables on the bottom
   are deeply browned and beginning to char in some places.
   (You will have to play around with the heat so that the
   vegetables aren't burned, crisp, and inedible).

2. Stir vegetables, then continue to cook without stirring
   for another 4 minutes, or until soft. Add garlic, tempeh,
   paprika, and cumin and cook, stirring constantly, for
   2 minutes. Add tomatoes with their juices and break up
   tomatoes using a wooden spoon. Reduce heat to medium-
   low and simmer for 10 minutes.

3. Add artichoke hearts and heat through. Taste and add salt
   and pepper if required.

   PAT'S TIP: Most of the smoky depth of flavor comes from the charred peppers
   and onion, but you don't want black, burnt vegetables. Even though you aren't
   stirring the vegetables, watch them carefully while they cook undisturbed. If you
   have a porcelain enamel nonstick skillet, use it. If using a cast-iron skillet, reduce heat
   to medium-low in step 1 after adding onion and peppers and cook for less time.

YOU'VE GOT OPTIONS

- Shakshuka originated in North Africa but has gained
  popularity throughout the Middle East, Western Europe, and
  North America. It typically incorporates fresh chile peppers,
  such as jalapeño, chipotle, or serrano. Or you can use red
  pepper flakes to your own preference.

- Cumin can be replaced with 1 tablespoon Garam Masala Spice
  Blend (page 25), or store-bought.

- Smoked paprika (usually Spanish) adds another layer of flavor
  to this dish, but you can swap it for sweet paprika.

MIXED VEGETABLE BAKE

MAKES 4 TO 6 SERVINGS, EASILY HALVED

TOPPING (SEE OPTIONS)

2 cloves garlic

¼ cup shelled raw sunflower seeds

2 slices bread, cubed

About ½ cup extra-virgin olive oil

VEGETABLE BAKE

4 cups mixed vegetables (see options)

2 medium potatoes, cut into cubes (see options)

1 medium onion, quartered

1 teaspoon sea salt

1 cup unflavored, unsweetened nondairy milk

⅓ cup cashews

Sea salt and pepper

1. Preheat oven to 350°F. Lightly oil an 8-cup ovenproof casserole dish.

2. Make topping: Combine garlic and sunflower seeds in the bowl of a small food processor. Process for 30 seconds, or until chopped together. Add bread, and with the motor running, add enough oil through opening in the lid to make a dry, crumbly mixture. Set aside.

3. Make vegetable bake: Combine mixed vegetables, potatoes, and onion in a large saucepan. Cover with water and add salt. Bring to a boil over high heat. Cover, reduce heat to medium-low, and simmer for 8 minutes, or until vegetables are almost tender (the tip of a knife should meet with some resistance when vegetables are pierced). Drain, reserving cooking liquid.

4. Meanwhile, combine milk and cashews in the jug of a blender. Blend on high for 2 minutes, or until nuts are completely puréed and cream is smooth. Scrape into a large bowl. Add cooked vegetables and mix well. Spoon into prepared casserole dish. Spread topping evenly over top. Bake for 30 minutes, or until topping is browned and vegetable mixture is bubbling. Grind salt and pepper over the top.

YOU'VE GOT OPTIONS

- The topping is really easy to make and it adds crunch, but to save time, you could use 1½ cups seasoned croutons or ½ cup Vegan Parmesan Cheese (page 39) instead.

- For the mixed vegetables, fresh is best but frozen will work. If using frozen vegetables, reduce the cooking time in step 3.

- Try to include 2 cups each of vegetables of the following colors:

  - **Green:** broccoli florets, coarsely chopped Swiss chard or kale or spinach or bok choy, lima beans or green peas, or 1-inch cut green beans, asparagus, or zucchini

  - **Red/orange/white:** 1-inch diced carrots, corn kernels, cauliflower florets, 1-inch diced parsnips or rutabaga

PORTOBELLO, POBLANO, AND PECAN FAJITAS

MAKES 6 FAJITAS

4 tablespoons extra-virgin avocado oil, divided

3 large portobello mushrooms, stemmed, halved, and sliced

1 clove garlic, chopped

1 jalapeño pepper, seeded and cut into thin strips

1 poblano pepper, seeded and sliced

1 red or green bell pepper, seeded and cut into ½-inch strips

1 medium onion, sliced

½ cup whole pecans (see options)

1 tablespoon coconut sugar

1 tablespoon Garam Masala Spice Blend (page 25), or store-bought

6 (6-inch) soft flour or corn tortillas

¾ cup Avocado Dip (page 45), or store-bought guacamole (see options)

6 tablespoons chopped fresh cilantro or parsley (optional)

Sea salt and pepper

1. Preheat oven to 300°F.

2. Heat 2 tablespoons of the oil in a large skillet over medium-high heat. Add mushrooms and garlic and cook, stirring frequently, for 6 minutes or until soft and tender. Remove to a plate and set aside.

3. Add jalapeño pepper, poblano pepper, bell pepper, and onion to the skillet with 1 tablespoon of the oil if required. Cook, stirring frequently, for 6 minutes, or until soft and tender. Remove to the plate with mushrooms and set aside.

4. Add pecans, sugar, and spice blend to the skillet with the remaining tablespoon of oil if required. Cook, stirring frequently, for 8 minutes, or until nuts are toasted. Add mushrooms, peppers, and their juices back to the skillet and heat through, stirring constantly (about 1 minute).

5. Meanwhile, heat tortillas: Wrap tortillas in a wet kitchen towel and place on center rack in preheated oven. Use within 5 minutes.

6. Working one at a time, spoon ¼ cup of the vegetable-nut mixture onto one half of the tortilla. Add 2 tablespoons avocado dip and garnish with 1 tablespoon chopped fresh cilantro (if using). Grind salt and pepper over the top. Fold in half to serve.

YOU'VE GOT OPTIONS

- If you like heat, add 1 chopped fresh chile pepper to the ingredients.

- In place of the pecans, try pistachios, Brazil nuts, or other nuts.

- In place of the avocado dip, add 2 slices fresh avocado to each tortilla, on top of the vegetable-nut mixture in step 6.

STUFFED SQUASH WITH LENTILS AND RICE

MAKES 4 SERVINGS

2 small butternut squash (see options)

3 tablespoons extra-virgin avocado oil, divided

1 cup long-grain brown or white rice

½ teaspoon sea salt

1 medium onion, chopped

½ cup pecan or walnut pieces

1 (14-ounce) can cooked lentils, drained

Sea salt and pepper

GARNISH (OPTIONAL)

½ cup Vegan Parmesan Cheese (page 39), or store-bought

1. Preheat oven to 375°F. Line a rimmed baking sheet with parchment paper.

2. Cut squash in half lengthwise. Remove and discard seeds. Cut the long, narrow "neck" end off each half, about an inch from the seed cup. Refrigerate neck ends for another meal. Brush the cut sides of the seed cups with 1 tablespoon of the oil and place cut side down on prepared baking sheet.

3. Bake for 25 minutes, or until tender when pierced with a knife.

4. Meanwhile, make filling: Combine rice with 2 cups water and salt in a saucepan. Bring to a boil over medium-high heat. Cover, reduce heat to medium-low, and simmer for 20 minutes, or until tender (all the water should be absorbed). Fluff with a fork and set aside.

5. Heat remaining oil in a skillet over medium-high heat. Add onion and pecans and cook, stirring frequently, for 5 minutes, or until onion is soft and pecans are toasted. Stir in lentils and heat through. Remove from heat and stir in rice. Season to taste with salt and pepper.

PAT'S TIP: Butternut squash is moist and firm and has a pleasant taste, and since you are only using the bulbous end, you will have enough squash left over to make Baked Squash Curry (page 174) another day.

YOU'VE GOT OPTIONS

You can use 2 small acorn squash instead of butternut squash for this recipe. Cut acorn squash in half, remove seeds, brush with oil, place cut side down on baking sheet, and proceed with step 3.

TO SERVE

Spoon stuffing into cooked squash cups. If desired, sprinkle 2 tablespoons vegan Parmesan cheese over each squash half. Serve immediately.

SWEET POTATO ENCHILADAS

MAKES 6 ENCHILADAS

SEE PHOTOGRAPH ON PAGE 192

1 medium sweet potato, peeled and cut into ½-inch dice

2 tablespoons extra-virgin avocado oil

1 red onion, chopped

1 red bell pepper, chopped

½ to 1 serrano pepper, chopped (optional)

3 cloves garlic, finely chopped

1 cup Tomato Salsa (page 78), or hot or mild store-bought salsa

2 cups chopped spinach (see options)

2 cups cooked or 1 (14-ounce) can black beans, rinsed and drained

Sea salt and pepper

2½ cups Enchilada Sauce, Try it! recipe (page 191) or store-bought, divided

8 (10-inch) soft flour or corn tortillas

GARNISH (OPTIONAL)

1 cup Avocado Dip (page 45), or store-bought guacamole

1 cup Vegan Yogurt (page 66), or store-bought

1 cup plus 2 tablespoons whole cashews

½ cup chopped fresh cilantro or parsley

1 tablespoon freshly squeezed lime juice

1. Preheat oven to 350°F. Lightly oil a rectangular baking dish (8 by 12 inches).

2. Bring a saucepan of salted water to a boil over high heat. Add sweet potato, reduce heat to medium-low, and simmer for 10 minutes, or until tender when pierced with a knife. Drain and set aside.

3. Meanwhile, make filling: Heat oil in a large skillet over medium-high heat. Add onion, bell pepper, and serrano pepper (if using) and cook, stirring frequently, for 5 minutes, or until soft. Add garlic and cook, stirring frequently, for 3 minutes.

4. Add salsa and bring to a simmer. Stir in spinach and beans and cook, stirring frequently, for 2 minutes, or until spinach is wilted. Remove from heat and stir in sweet potato. Season to taste with salt and pepper.

5. Spread 1 cup of the enchilada sauce evenly in prepared baking dish.

6. Fill tortillas: Working one at a time, spoon ½ cup sweet potato in the center of the tortilla to within 1 inch of the edges. Fold tortilla top and bottom over the filling. Then fold the right side over the filling and spin the tortilla one-quarter turn to the right so that the filling is closest to you. Using two hands, gently pull the covered filling toward you to make a tight roll. Roll filled half of the tortilla away from you and over the rest of the tortilla and place it, seam side down, in baking dish. Fill and roll remaining tortillas, placing them seam side down in baking dish.

7. Spread remaining 1½ cups of enchilada sauce evenly over the top of the enchiladas and bake for 20 minutes, or until sauce is bubbling and enchiladas are heated through.

YOU'VE GOT OPTIONS

- Any green such as kale, Swiss chard, or bok choy will work in place of the spinach.

- For extra protein, you can add 1 (8- to 10-ounce) package tempeh, thawed if frozen and cut into ½-inch dice, to the pan with the garlic in step 3. This increases the amount of filling to fill 8 to 10 enchiladas.

Try it! ENCHILADA SAUCE

MAKES ABOUT 2½ CUPS

1 (4- or 5-ounce) jar roasted red bell peppers, drained

1 cup Vegan Mayonnaise (page 43), or store-bought

1 clove garlic, minced

1 jalapeño pepper, finely chopped

1 cup Tomato Salsa (page 78), or store-bought

¼ cup golden raisins, finely chopped

½ teaspoon ground cinnamon

¼ teaspoon ground allspice

1. Finely chop roasted peppers and set aside in a strainer or small colander in the sink to drain.

2. Combine mayonnaise, garlic, jalapeño pepper, salsa, raisins, cinnamon, and allspice in a medium-sized bowl. Stir in drained peppers.

Sweet Potato Enchiladas, page 190

Veggie Pot Pie, page 194

VEGGIE POT PIE

MAKES 4 TO 6 SERVINGS

SEE PHOTOGRAPH ON PAGE 193

2 tablespoons extra-virgin avocado oil

1 medium onion, chopped

½ red bell pepper, chopped

1 clove garlic, chopped

1 tablespoon Mediterranean Herb Blend (page 147), or store-bought

¼ cup unflavored, unsweetened nondairy milk

3 tablespoons cornstarch

2 cups Vegetable Broth (page 125), or store-bought

2 cups chopped fresh mixed vegetables (see options)

1 batch Vegan Pie Pastry, Try it! recipe (page 195), or 1 package store-bought regular or gluten-free pie pastry, thawed (see options)

1. Preheat oven to 425°F. Lightly oil four large or six medium-sized ovenproof ramekins or small bowls, or one 8 by 8-inch baking dish, and place on a rimmed baking sheet.

2. Heat oil in a saucepan over medium-high heat. Add onion and pepper and cook, stirring frequently, for 5 minutes, or until soft. Add garlic and herb blend and cook, stirring frequently, for 3 minutes.

3. Combine milk and cornstarch in a small bowl. Whisk vigorously to mix into a smooth paste. Set aside.

4. Add broth to the saucepan and bring to a boil. Stir in cornstarch paste, reduce heat, and simmer, stirring constantly, for about 10 minutes, or until liquid is thickened.

5. Add vegetables and simmer for about 10 minutes, or until tender when pierced with the tip of a knife.

6. Meanwhile, roll pastry to ¼ inch thick and cut out four or six rounds slightly smaller than the size of the ramekins , or shape into an 8 by 8-inch square.

7. Ladle vegetables and liquid into ramekins or baking dish and top with pastry. Bake for 15 minutes, or until pastry is browned and liquid is bubbly.

TO SERVE

Let pot pie(s) stand for 5 minutes to cool slightly before serving.

YOU'VE GOT OPTIONS

- As an alternative to pastry topping, cut circles, triangles, or squares from soft tortillas, naan bread, or baked pizza dough, brush with extra-virgin olive oil, and use them to top the pies.

- The recipe calls for 2 cups chopped mixed vegetables. Use carrots, parsnips, potatoes, peas, corn, Brussels sprouts, or beets. Or use frozen mixed vegetables to save prep time. Add frozen vegetables in step 5 and simmer for about 5 or 6 minutes, until tender when pierced with the tip of a knife.

Try it! VEGAN PIE PASTRY

MAKES 1 (12-INCH) PIE SHELL

1½ cups unbleached all-purpose flour, plus more for rolling

1 teaspoon granulated sugar

½ teaspoon sea salt

½ cup extra-virgin coconut oil, chilled (see tips)

4 to 5 tablespoons unflavored, unsweetened almond milk, chilled

PAT'S TIPS: Do not use melted coconut oil in this recipe. The key to making flaky pastry is to use oil that is firm, yet soft enough to scoop into a ½-cup dry measuring cup. Best results are achieved if you measure ½ cup softened coconut oil and then chill it in the refrigerator.

You can double the recipe, cut two equal portions of dough, and roll out a pie bottom and a top. Or, if you only need one portion, you can wrap the second portion tightly, label, and freeze for up to 3 months. Thaw in the refrigerator before rolling.

1. Chill a rolling pin and a pastry cloth or kitchen towel in the refrigerator until ready to roll out the pastry.

2. Combine flour, sugar, and salt in a large bowl. Add oil and use a pastry cutter or two knives to cut the oil into the flour (the mixture should look like rolled oats). Cut, don't mash, the oil into the flour.

3. Sprinkle 2 tablespoons of the milk over the mixture and blend using a fork. Add more milk, 1 tablespoon at a time, and blend until the mixture comes together to form a soft ball. Don't overmix or knead the dough. Wrap the dough in plastic and chill for 12 to 15 minutes in the refrigerator.

4. Roll the pastry: Spread chilled pastry cloth over your workspace and sprinkle lightly with flour. Position chilled dough in the center of the cloth and pat it into a square or circle using your hands. Roll the dough out evenly to ¼ inch thick. You should have a rectangle that measures about 10 by 12 inches or a circle about 12 inches in diameter.

   For Pies: Line a pie pan with the pastry, press into the bottom and up the sides of the pan, and trim away excess dough around the top of the pan.

   For Tarts: Cut circles that measure 1 to 2 inches larger than the tart pan wells, press into the bottom and up the sides of the wells, and trim away excess dough around the top of the wells.

   For Pot Pies: Cut circles that measure ¼ to ½ inch smaller than the pot pie bowls and position over the filled pot pie bowls.

Apple Crisp, page 198

DESSERTS AND SWEET TREATS

APPLE CRISP

SEE PHOTOGRAPH ON PAGE 196

⅓ cup softened extra-virgin coconut oil

1 cup coconut sugar

1 cup rolled oats

½ cup pecans or walnuts, chopped

½ teaspoon ground cinnamon

¼ teaspoon sea salt

5 or 6 apples (Macintosh, Gala, or any crisp, tart apple)

2 tablespoons freshly squeezed lemon juice

FOR SERVING (OPTIONAL)

French Vanilla Ice Cream, Try it! recipe (page 199) or store-bought

TO SERVE

Spoon apples and topping into individual serving dishes and serve with French vanilla ice cream, if desired.

1. Preheat oven to 375°F. Lightly oil a 1½-quart square or round baking dish.

2. Beat together oil and sugar in a bowl using a wooden spoon. Add oats, walnuts, cinnamon, and salt and stir to evenly distribute. The mixture will be thick and crumbly. Set aside.

3. Peel, core, and slice the apples into the prepared baking dish, until they fill roughly two-thirds of the dish. Sprinkle with lemon juice and toss to combine.

4. Spoon oat mixture on top of the apples, spreading it around to cover them. Bake for 40 minutes, or until apples are tender and topping is golden brown and crisp.

Try it!
FRENCH VANILLA ICE CREAM

MAKES 4 TO 6 SERVINGS

SEE PHOTOGRAPH ON PAGE 200

2 (13.5-ounce) cans full-fat coconut milk

1 fresh vanilla pod (see options)

⅔ cup corn syrup or pure maple syrup

1 tablespoon pure vanilla extract

½ teaspoon kosher salt or coarsely ground sea salt

1. **Day Before:** Set the ice cream maker bowl in the freezer.

2. Open one can of coconut milk. Split the vanilla bean in half. Run the tip of a paring knife up and down the inside of each pod half to collect the tiny black seeds and scrape them into the coconut milk.

3. Combine both cans coconut milk, corn syrup, vanilla extract, and salt in the jug of a blender. Process for 30 seconds, or until smooth. Scrape into a batter bowl or 4-cup liquid measuring cup. Cover tightly and refrigerate overnight.

4. **Next Day:** Pour chilled mixture into ice cream maker bowl and process, following manufacturer's instructions, for about 20 minutes, or until thick and creamy.

TO USE

Scoop immediately and enjoy as soft ice cream. You can add flavorings such as ¼ cup halved cherries; ½ cup semisweet chocolate chips; or ¼ cup chopped fresh peaches.

TO STORE

Transfer to a loaf pan (8½ by 4½ inches) or freezerproof container, cover tightly, and freeze for 4 to 5 hours, or until firm. Set out at room temperature for 20 minutes to soften before using. Keep in the freezer for up to 3 days.

YOU'VE GOT OPTIONS

- A real vanilla pod is the ingredient that takes this ice cream from ordinary to *French*. Look for vanilla pods in specialty stores or in the baking ingredients aisle of your supermarket. Because they are expensive, don't throw away the pod halves once you have scraped out the seeds. Instead, break them into 1- to 2-inch pieces and add to your sugar canister to impart a slight vanilla flavor.

- If you don't have a vanilla pod but have the urge for vanilla ice cream, increase the amount of pure vanilla extract to 2 tablespoons.

French Vanilla Ice Cream, page 199

Brownies, page 202

BROWNIES

MAKES 16 (2-INCH) SQUARES

SEE PHOTOGRAPH ON PAGE 201

⅓ cup unflavored, unsweetened almond milk or other nondairy milk

3 tablespoons flaxseeds

1 cup all-purpose flour or gluten-free flour blend

½ cup unsweetened cocoa powder

1 teaspoon baking powder

½ teaspoon sea salt

¾ cup coconut sugar

5 tablespoons softened extra-virgin coconut oil

3 tablespoons applesauce

1 teaspoon pure vanilla extract

½ cup coarsely chopped pecans (optional)

½ cup coarsely chopped vegan semisweet chocolate or carob (see tips)

1. Preheat oven to 350°F. Lightly oil an 8-inch square baking pan.

2. Whisk milk and flaxseeds together in a small bowl using a fork and set aside.

3. Combine flour, cocoa, baking powder, and salt in a medium-sized bowl. Whisk to mix and set aside.

4. Beat together sugar and oil in a large bowl using a wooden spoon. Add applesauce and vanilla and beat until the mixture is soft and creamy. Add milk mixture and beat to mix well.

5. Stir in half of the flour mixture (dry ingredients) and beat to mix well. Add remaining dry ingredients and stir to mix well. Stir in pecans (if using) and chocolate pieces.

6. Scrape into prepared pan and spread evenly. Bake for 35 to 45 minutes, until a toothpick inserted into the center comes out clean. Set aside to cool in the pan. Cut into 2-inch squares.

PAT'S TIPS: If you store chocolate chips or pieces in the freezer and add them frozen to cake or brownie batter, they will melt during baking but will remain in place, providing small pockets of pure chocolate in the finished product.

The longer brownies cook, the drier and more cake-like they become. So if you check the brownies a couple of minutes before the minimum time given and there is crumbly (not wet) batter clinging to the toothpick, remove the brownies from the oven and they will be chewy, not dry.

TO STORE

Store brownies in a container with a tight-fitting lid in the refrigerator for up to 1 week.

CARO-BARK

6 tablespoons coconut sugar

6 tablespoons coconut oil

6 tablespoons carob or cocoa powder

¼ cup coarsely chopped almonds (see options)

¼ cup dried cranberries (see options)

½ teaspoon kosher salt or coarsely ground sea salt (optional)

1. Line a baking sheet with parchment paper.

2. Grind the sugar to a fine powder in a coffee or spice grinder. You can skip this step, but if you do, the sugar won't blend into the oil and the texture of the bark will be slightly gritty.

3. Melt oil in a saucepan over medium-low heat. Stir in the coconut sugar and carob powder. Pour onto the prepared sheet and sprinkle with almonds, cranberries, and salt (if using). Refrigerate for about 10 minutes, or until set.

TO STORE

Break up chilled bark roughly into 2-inch pieces. Store in a parchment-lined airtight container in the refrigerator for up to 4 weeks or in a freezer bag in the freezer for up to 2 months.

YOU'VE GOT OPTIONS

You have lots of room to be creative with this recipe. Use dried blueberries; chopped, dried apricots; chopped, candied ginger; or other fruit in place of the cranberries and try different nuts. Or make it decadent and sprinkle caramel or peanut butter chips over top.

CHOCOLATE CHIP COOKIES

MAKES 2 DOZEN SMALL (2-INCH) COOKIES

¼ cup unflavored, unsweetened almond milk or other nondairy milk

2 tablespoons flaxseeds

1 cup all-purpose flour or gluten-free flour blend

½ teaspoon baking powder

¼ teaspoon sea salt

¾ cup coconut sugar

½ cup softened coconut oil

1 teaspoon pure vanilla extract

1 cup vegan semisweet chocolate chips

1. Adjust an oven rack to the center of the oven and preheat oven to 350°F. Line two baking sheets with parchment paper.

2. Combine almond milk and flaxseeds in a small bowl. Whisk with a fork to mix and set aside.

3. Combine flour, baking powder, and salt in a medium-sized bowl. Whisk to mix and set aside.

4. In a large bowl, beat together the sugar and oil using a wooden spoon. Add vanilla and the milk mixture and stir to mix. Add flour mixture and stir just until combined (make sure there are no dry ingredients in the bottom of the bowl). Stir in chocolate chips.

5. Drop heaping tablespoon-size balls of dough about 2 inches apart on one of the prepared baking sheets. If you have one, use a small ice cream scoop to keep the size of the cookies uniform. Bake on center rack for 8 to 10 minutes, until cookies are lightly browned on bottom and firm on the top. Set aside on the pan to cool slightly, then transfer cookies to a plate or cooling rack using a spatula. Set aside to cool completely.

6. While the first batch of cookies is baking, drop dough on the second baking sheet. While the first batch cools, bake the second batch as directed. Keep dropping and baking cookies, rotating baking sheets, until all of the dough has been used.

PAT'S TIPS: Trying to juggle two baking sheets in the oven at the same time may cause cookies to burn on the bottom or be undercooked on the top. Best to load and bake one baking sheet at a time. Load the second sheet while the first is baking and pop in the oven when the first sheet comes out.

The longer cookies bake, the drier and more cake-like they become. For chewy cookies, check them a couple of minutes before the minimum baking time given. If there is crumbly (not wet) batter clinging to the toothpick, remove cookies from the oven.

TO STORE

Transfer cooled cookies to an airtight container. Cookies will keep at room temperature for up to 1 week and frozen for up to 3 months.

YOU'VE GOT OPTIONS

- Using coconut flour makes these cookies gluten-free, but they will be more fragile than if you use all-purpose flour.

- Cookies do firm up upon cooling but are still crumbly, which makes them perfect for topping puddings and other desserts, such as Easy Lemon Mess (page 210).

CHOCOLATE CUPCAKES

MAKES 1 DOZEN CUPCAKES

SEE PHOTOGRAPH ON PAGES 208–209

1 cup unflavored, unsweetened almond milk or other nondairy milk

6 tablespoons extra-virgin olive oil

1 tablespoon balsamic vinegar

1 teaspoon pure vanilla extract

1½ cups all-purpose flour or gluten-free flour blend

1 cup coconut sugar

¼ cup cocoa powder

1 teaspoon baking powder

1 teaspoon espresso powder (optional)

½ teaspoon baking soda

½ teaspoon sea salt

¾ cup Chocolate Icing, Try it! recipe (page 207) or store-bought

1. Preheat oven to 350°F. Line a 12-well muffin pan with paper cups or lightly oil.

2. Measure milk in a 2-cup liquid measuring cup. Whisk in oil, vinegar, and vanilla using a fork. Set aside.

3. Whisk together flour, sugar, cocoa powder, baking powder, espresso powder (if using), baking soda, and salt in a large bowl.

4. Add milk mixture and beat using a wooden spoon until the batter is smooth. Spoon batter into prepared muffin pan, filling the wells almost to the top. Bake for 20 minutes, or until a toothpick inserted into the middle of a cupcake comes out clean. Cool in the pan for 5 minutes and transfer to a cooling rack to cool completely.

5. Grasp a cupcake by the bottom, turn upside down, dip into the icing, and twist to coat the top. Place on a plate and repeat for remaining cupcakes.

TO STORE

Cupcakes keep in an airtight container in the refrigerator for up to 1 week.

Try it!
CHOCOLATE ICING

MAKES ABOUT ¾ CUP

½ cup softened extra-virgin coconut oil

¼ cup pure maple syrup

3 tablespoons cocoa or carob powder

Pinch of sea salt

Combine oil and maple syrup in a medium-sized bowl. Beat using a wooden spoon. Add cocoa and salt and beat to combine.

TO USE

Icing will harden slightly upon chilling, so use while it is soft. *For cupcakes:* Grasp a cupcake by the bottom, turn upside down, dip into the icing, and twist to coat the top. Place on a plate and repeat for remaining cupcakes. *For bars or cakes:* Spoon icing on top of bars or cake. Spread evenly over the top using a metal spatula.

TO STORE

Icing keeps in an airtight container in the refrigerator for up to 1 month. Bring to room temperature before using.

Chocolate Cupcakes, page 206, and Chocolate Icing, page 207

EASY LEMON MESS

1 batch Easy Lemon Curd, Try it! recipe
(page 211) or store-bought

1 cup fresh strawberries, hulled and
quartered (see options)

GARNISH (OPTIONAL)

½ cup Coconut Whipped Cream
(page 213), or store-bought

½ cup French Vanilla Ice Cream
(page 199), or store-bought

For each serving, spoon ½ cup lemon curd into a glass or
sundae cup. Spoon ¼ cup strawberries over curd and spoon
about 2 tablespoons whipped cream or ice cream on top (if
using).

YOU'VE GOT OPTIONS

- This dessert is popular in England, where it's called Eton Mess. Instead of using lemon curd, combine
  2 cups sliced fresh strawberries with 1½ to 2 cups softened French Vanilla Ice Cream (page 199), or
  store-bought.

- And for real decadence, sprinkle 1 tablespoon vegan semisweet chocolate pieces over the top of each
  serving.

Try it!
EASY LEMON CURD

MAKES 2 CUPS

2 lemons

¾ cup granulated sugar

1 tablespoon softened extra-virgin coconut oil

3 tablespoons cornstarch

3 tablespoons nutritional yeast

Pinch of sea salt

TO STORE
Transfer curd to a 2-cup-capacity jar or container with a lid and keep in the refrigerator for up to 1 week.

1. Grate the zest from half of 1 lemon using a small grater (you should have about 2 tablespoons) and set aside. Be careful to take only the yellow rind, avoiding the white pith. Juice both lemons (you should have about ½ cup) and set aside.

2. Process zest and sugar in the bowl of a food processor for 1 minute. Add oil, cornstarch, and yeast and process for 30 seconds to combine. Add the lemon juice, 1½ cups water, and salt and process for 20 seconds, or until mixed.

3. Pour the mixture into a saucepan and cook over low heat, stirring constantly, for 7 minutes, or until thickened. Keep the mixture simmering, not boiling, as it cooks. Remove from heat and set aside in the pan to cool completely. Chill for at least 30 minutes in the refrigerator. Curd thickens upon cooling.

PUMPKIN PIE

MAKES 1 (9- OR 10-INCH) PIE

1 batch Vegan Pie Pastry (page 195), or 1 package store-bought regular or gluten-free pie pastry, thawed

⅓ cup pure maple syrup

⅓ cup unflavored, unsweetened or vanilla almond milk

¼ cup coconut sugar

3 tablespoons cornstarch

1 tablespoon extra-virgin olive oil

2 teaspoons pumpkin pie spice (see options)

¼ teaspoon sea salt

2 (15-ounce) cans pumpkin purée or 3 cups cooked pumpkin purée (see options)

FOR SERVING (OPTIONAL)

1 cup Coconut Whipped Cream, Try it! recipe (page 213) or store-bought

1 batch French Vanilla Ice Cream (page 199), or 1 quart store-bought

1. Preheat oven to 350°F.

2. Roll pastry to ¼ inch thick. Wrap around rolling pin and transfer to a 9- or 10-inch pie pan. Press pastry into bottom and sides and trim away excess. Set aside.

3. Make filling: Combine maple syrup, milk, sugar, cornstarch, oil, spice, salt, and pumpkin purée in the jug of a blender. Process for 1 minute, or until smooth, scraping down sides of the jug once or twice. Pour filling into pie shell and bake for 1 hour. Filling should be firm and lightly browned (it may have some cracks) and pastry should be browned.

TO SERVE

Set aside to cool for 1 hour before slicing. You can cover cooled pie and refrigerate overnight to firm up the pie filling, but bring back to room temperature before serving.

Slice and serve with a dollop of coconut whipped cream or ice cream (if using).

YOU'VE GOT OPTIONS

Make your own pumpkin pie spice. Here's how: Combine 3 tablespoons ground cinnamon, 2 teaspoons ground allspice, 2 teaspoons ground nutmeg, 1 teaspoon ground cloves, and 1 teaspoon ground ginger. Makes about ¼ cup. Transfer to a small jar, label and cap with lid. Spices keep in a cool, dark cupboard for up to 1 year.

Try it!
COCONUT WHIPPED CREAM

MAKES ABOUT 2½ CUPS

1 (13.5-ounce) can coconut cream or full-fat coconut milk

½ cup confectioners' sugar, divided

½ teaspoon pure vanilla extract

TO STORE

Use immediately or scrape into a container with a lid and keep in the refrigerator for up to 1 week. Coconut whipped cream hardens in the refrigerator.

1. **Night Before:** Chill coconut cream and a large mixing bowl in the refrigerator overnight. Do not shake or tip the can; you want to allow the solids and liquid to separate and use only the solids for making whipped cream.

2. **Next Day:** Open can of coconut cream without shaking and lift out solid, thick cream at the top, discarding liquid or reserving for another use. Transfer cream to chilled bowl. Beat for 30 seconds using electric mixer or wand. Sprinkle ¼ cup of the sugar over the cream, add vanilla, and beat for 30 seconds. Sprinkle in remaining ¼ cup of sugar and beat for about 1 minute, or until soft peaks form.

PAT'S TIP: Use coconut cream or full-fat coconut milk because it is the solid coconut oil that whips into a cream-like product. Sometimes, if there is too much liquid in the solid cream, you won't be able to get a whipped cream. If this happens, add 2 to 4 tablespoons tapioca flour or cornstarch as you whip. Refrigerating the mixture helps to solidify it.

ROASTED STRAWBERRY RHUBARB SUNDAE

MAKES 4 SUNDAES

1 batch French Vanilla Ice Cream (page 199), or 1 quart store-bought ice cream, softened

2 cups Roasted Strawberry Rhubarb Sauce, Try it! recipe (page 215) (see options)

1 cup fresh strawberries, hulled

Scoop ice cream into four sundae dishes or bowls. Ladle ½ cup of sauce over each serving and garnish with fresh strawberries.

YOU'VE GOT OPTIONS

- Any preserved fruit or compote makes a delicious sundae topping, so if strawberry-rhubarb sauce is not available, look for strawberry, grape, plum, apricot, mango, or peach preserves to use as a topping.

- You can also use jam as a topping. The difference between jam and preserves is that jam is usually made with crushed fruit so that it is spreadable, whereas preserves contain whole or large chunks of fruit.

Try it!
ROASTED STRAWBERRY RHUBARB SAUCE

MAKES ABOUT 3 CUPS

2 cups chopped fresh rhubarb (about ½ pound) (see options)

2 cups chopped fresh strawberries (about ½ pound) (see options)

½ cup coconut sugar

2 tablespoons orange juice

1 teaspoon extra-virgin coconut oil

1. Preheat oven to 375°F.

2. Combine rhubarb, strawberries, sugar, juice, and oil in an 8-inch square or oval baking dish. Toss to mix well. Roast, stirring once, for 30 minutes, or until fruit is tender and juices have thickened. Set aside to cool completely.

TO STORE
Rhubarb sauce keeps in a covered container in the refrigerator for up to 2 weeks.

YOU'VE GOT OPTIONS

Springtime is when the tartness of fresh rhubarb is complemented by the sweetness of strawberries and we enjoy their combination in pies, tarts, compotes, and preserves. This sauce is best if made with fresh fruit.

SPICED OATMEAL COOKIES

MAKES ABOUT 2 DOZEN COOKIES

2 tablespoons ground flaxseeds

½ cup unflavored, unsweetened or vanilla nondairy milk, divided

1 cup rolled oats

¾ cup spelt flour (see options)

½ teaspoon baking powder

½ teaspoon baking soda

¼ teaspoon ground allspice

¼ teaspoon ground cinnamon

¼ teaspoon sea salt

⅔ cup coconut sugar

½ cup softened extra-virgin coconut oil

½ teaspoon pure vanilla extract

½ cup vegan semisweet chocolate chips (optional)

1. Position an oven rack in the center of the oven and preheat oven to 400°F. Lightly oil two baking sheets.

2. Combine ground flaxseeds and 3 tablespoons of the milk in a medium-sized bowl. Set aside for 10 minutes.

3. Combine rolled oats, flour, baking powder, baking soda, allspice, cinnamon, and salt in a large bowl and whisk with a fork to mix well. Set aside.

4. Combine sugar, oil, and vanilla in a large bowl and cream together using a wooden spoon. Beat in flaxseed mixture. Sprinkle in half of the flour mixture and beat to mix well. Add the remaining 5 tablespoons of milk and beat to mix well. Sprinkle in remaining flour mixture and beat to mix well. Mix in chocolate chips (if using).

5. Scoop about 2 tablespoons of cookie dough and drop onto one of the prepared baking sheets. Repeat, leaving about 2 inches between cookies, until baking sheet is full. Bake for 8 minutes, or until lightly browned. Remove and let sit for 7 minutes, or until firm enough to remove to a cooling rack.

6. While the first batch of cookies is baking, drop remaining cookie dough on the second baking sheet. While the first batch cools, bake second batch as directed.

TO STORE

Cookies keep in an airtight container in the refrigerator for up to 1 week.

YOU'VE GOT OPTIONS

- Using spelt flour, coconut flour, or a gluten-free flour blend produces cookies that are thin, lacy, and crisp. If you use all-purpose flour, the cookies will not spread as much during cooking and they will be denser and firmer.

- Add ¼ cup raisins, if desired, with chocolate chips in step 4.

WARM BANANA SPLIT

MAKES 4 SERVINGS

2 bananas

Juice of ½ lemon

2 tablespoons coconut sugar

1 tablespoon extra-virgin avocado oil

1 teaspoon ground cinnamon (optional)

4 scoops French Vanilla Ice Cream
(page 199), or store-bought

¼ cup caramel sauce

¼ cup chocolate sauce

¼ cup peach preserves

¼ cup strawberry preserves or Roasted
Strawberry Rhubarb Sauce (page 215)

GARNISH (OPTIONAL)

½ cup chopped nuts

½ cup shredded coconut

4 whole maraschino cherries

1. Position an oven rack on the top rung and preheat oven to broil. Line a baking sheet with parchment paper.

2. Peel and cut the bananas into 1-inch chunks. Combine bananas, lemon juice, sugar, oil, and cinnamon (if using) together in a bowl and toss to coat. Spread in one layer on prepared baking sheet, scraping liquids over evenly. Broil on top rack in oven for 1 minute, stir, and broil for 30 seconds, or until sugar is bubbling.

3. Divide bananas evenly among four dessert bowls. Scoop ice cream into each bowl and top one with caramel sauce, one with chocolate sauce, one with peach preserves, and one with strawberry preserves.

TO SERVE

If desired, garnish each bowl with nuts, coconut, and/or cherries, or pass garnishes separately.

YOU'VE GOT OPTIONS

This is an updated version of the old-fashioned banana split. If you really want a decadent dessert, here's how: Split the bananas in half lengthwise and arrange, cut sides down, on prepared baking sheet. Brush with oil, sprinkle with lemon juice, sugar, and cinnamon, and broil until sugar is bubbling. Arrange two halves in a bowl or banana split dish. Place 2 scoops of ice cream between the banana halves and top each scoop with one of the toppings. Garnish as desired. Repeat for remaining 2 banana halves. Makes two servings.

PEANUT BUTTER AND CHOCOLATE CREAM PIE

MAKES 8 TO 10 SERVINGS

CRUST (SEE OPTIONS)

1 cup pitted dates

1 cup almonds or pecans

¼ cup rolled oats

3 tablespoons cocoa powder

1 tablespoon softened coconut oil

1 cup vegan semisweet chocolate chips

FILLING

12 ounces firm silken tofu, slightly drained and patted dry

½ cup creamy salted peanut butter

¼ cup pure maple syrup (see options)

1 (13.5-ounce) can coconut cream or full-fat coconut milk

⅓ cup roasted and salted peanuts, roughly chopped (optional)

GARNISH (OPTIONAL)

½ cup vegan semisweet chocolate chips

1. **Night Before:** Chill coconut cream in refrigerator overnight.

2. **Next Day:** Preheat oven to 375°F. Lightly oil a 9- or 10-inch ovenproof glass pie pan.

3. Make crust: Process dates for 1 minute in a food processor, until roughly chopped. Add almonds and process for 1 minute, or until finely chopped. Add oats, cocoa, and oil and pulse to combine. Scrape into prepared pie pan and use the back of a spoon to press evenly over the bottom and up the sides of the pan. Bake for 10 minutes. Sprinkle chocolate chips evenly over bottom and set aside on a cooling rack to cool completely (chocolate will melt slightly). Chill in the refrigerator for 30 minutes, or you can make crust a day ahead and store, covered, in the refrigerator.

4. Make filling: Combine tofu, peanut butter, and maple syrup in the jug of a blender or food processor bowl and blend on high for 1 minute, or until smooth.

5. Scoop solid cream out of the coconut cream into a chilled bowl, discarding watery liquid or reserving for another use. Whip, using a fork, until a cream-like texture is achieved. Fold peanut butter mixture into whipped coconut cream. Cover and place in the freezer.

6. When crust is chilled, spread peanuts (if using) evenly over the chocolate on the bottom. Pour peanut butter filling over the peanuts and spread evenly using a spatula.

TO SERVE

Cover and freeze for 15 minutes before serving, or store in the freezer for up to 4 days (allow to stand for 3 hours at room temperature before serving). Garnish top of pie with chocolate chips if desired.

YOU'VE GOT OPTIONS

* For a traditional crust, use 1 batch Vegan Pie Pastry (page 195), or 1 package regular or gluten-free pie pastry, thawed, in place of crust ingredients. Roll pastry to ¼ inch thick, wrap around rolling pin, and transfer to a 9- or 10-inch pie pan. Press pastry into bottom and sides and trim away excess. Bake and add chocolate chips as in step 3.

* Maple syrup lends an almost caramel flavor to the filling, but you can use coconut or agave nectar instead.

* Try adding fresh bananas to the filling. Here's how: In step 6, slice 2 ripe but firm bananas and spread slices evenly over peanuts (if using). Pour peanut butter filling over the bananas and spread evenly using a spatula.

ACKNOWLEDGMENTS

This book would not have been possible without the generosity and encouragement of countless immensely committed and talented people. At the top of that list is Pat Crocker, for her fountain of knowledge and relentless commitment to creating recipes that make taste buds sing, as well as Ashleigh Amoroso, for her unparalleled photography skills, which brought the book to life. We three make a great team.

Words cannot express my appreciation for my fearless literary agent, Linda Konner, for her superb instincts, razor-sharp skills, and sage advice. For her consistent dedication and limitless talents, I am eternally grateful.

To the entire team at FaithWords and Center Street, a division of Hachette Book Group, I would like to share my deepest gratitude for believing in the book. Thank you to my editor, Virginia Bhashkar, for overseeing all facets of the publishing process; to Kallie Shimek and Erin Granville, for their masterful work in polishing the manuscript; to my team of marketing gurus, including Laini Brown, Sarah Falter, Patsy Jones, Rudy Kisch, and Katie Connors, for pulling out all the stops to successfully market and publicize the book; and to Laura Klynstra, for designing a beautiful cover and interior.

Thank you to Carlyn Cowen for being my go-to confidant and cocaptain in steering the Reducetarian Foundation. Your tremendous efforts and ongoing support (often going above and beyond) mean a great deal to me. I look forward to our continued partnership.

I'm grateful for the humor, kindness, and loyalty of my dearest friends, including but not limited to Michael Young, Isabella Cardona, Dan Feldman, Danielle Medina, David DiLillo, Joe Eastman, Tyler Alterman, Arthur Kapetanakis, Michael Trollan, Lauren Deaderick, Vincent Romano, Crichton Atkinson, and Sofia Davis-Fogel. I'm very lucky to have you all in my life.

Thank you to all our supporters and partners at the Reducetarian Foundation, who work every day to advance our shared mission for a more sustainable, healthy, and compassionate world. I'm in awe of what we have accomplished together and cannot wait to see what we do next.

I'd like to express my gratitude for Simba, whom I miss dearly and will never forget, and for Tobey, whose snuggles and licks bring me unmatched joy and laughter.

Thank you to Carolyn and Michael Hittleman for always making me feel like a part of the family.

I owe my parents—Linda and Russell Kateman—an eternal debt of gratitude for their practiced patience and unwavering support. The older I become, the more I glimpse a truer meaning of parenthood, and with that knowledge comes a deeper sense of respect and admiration for you both. I love you both very much.

And finally, to Isabel (my fiancée!): You are the most beautiful, intelligent, and capable being I know. I appreciate you and every quality about you that makes you, you. I'm an infinitely happier and better person because you are in my life. Your compassion, love, understanding, patience, and support mean the world to me. Know that whenever you want Buffalo cauliflower, I'll be in the kitchen preparing it for you (and I promise I'll remember to clean the dishes afterward). You are, and always will be, my #1.

BRIAN

INDEX

Page numbers of photographs appear in italics.

ABOUT THE AUTHOR

BRIAN KATEMAN is cofounder and president of the Reducetarian Foundation, a non-profit organization dedicated to reducing consumption of meat, eggs, and dairy to create a healthy, sustainable, and compassionate world. Brian is the editor of *The Reducetarian Solution*. His writings have appeared in dozens of media outlets including *The Atlantic*, *Quartz*, the *Los Angeles Times*, the *San Francisco Chronicle*, the *Washington Post*, *Vox*, and the *New York Daily News*. He is an instructor in the Executive Education Program at the Earth Institute Center for Environmental Sustainability at Columbia University. He lives in New York City with his fiancée, Isabel, and rescue dog, Tobey.